To:

Diane

May the Lord of peace himself
give you peace at all times and
in every way.

2 THESSALONIANS 3:16

from:

Jodi

Requests for information should be addressed to:
Inspirio, the gift group of Zondervan
Grand Rapids, Michigan 49530
http://www.inspiriogifts.com

Compiler: Robin Schmitt
Editor: Janice Jacobson
Design Manager: Amy J. Wenger
Designer: Peterman Design

Printed in China

04 05/ HK/ 5 4 3

Peace
for a
WOMAN'S SOUL

*Finding Rest for
Your Spirit*

ψ
inspirio™

Table of

Contents

The Peace of God

**BEYOND
UNDERSTANDING**

PEACE THAT PASSES UNDERSTANDING

I don't have any way of knowing where you are as you're reading this, but wherever it is in the whole wide earth, please know you are loved by the God of the universe. He offers you friendship and peace. He wants to share with you everything he has! His fellowship reaches next door, down the street, through the city, over the plains, across the ocean, and around the world.

Luci Swindoll

I will make a covenant of peace with them ... so that they may live in the desert and sleep in the forests in safety. I will bless them and the places surrounding my hill. I will send down showers in season; there will be showers of blessing. The trees of the field will yield their fruit and the ground will yield its crops; the people will be secure in their land.

EZEKIEL 34:25–27

The LORD bless you
   and keep you;
the LORD make his face shine upon you
   and be gracious to you;
the LORD turn his face toward you
   and give you peace.

NUMBERS 6:24–26

The above words may be familiar because this blessing is still pronounced in many churches today. But do you grasp its full magnitude? Do you realize who is speaking? It is the Lord, the Creator. His very name and character guarantee that he can give the promised peace. He graciously wants to bestow this on us.

Peace is a gift. It is given to those who want to accept it and who meet its conditions. Peace can never be separated from a personal relationship with God. It branches out to all aspects of our lives.

The offer of peace can be trusted. God is its guarantee. Whether we personally enjoy this peace is entirely in our own hands. God extends the offer. The acceptance depends on us.

Gien Karssen

MEDITATIONS ON PEACE THAT PASSES UNDERSTANDING

The LORD gives strength to his people;
the LORD blesses his people with peace.

PSALM 29:11

God promises peace to his people, his saints.

PSALM 85:8

"My people will live in peaceful dwelling places,
in secure homes,
in undisturbed places of rest,"
declares the LORD.

ISAIAH 32:18

The meek will inherit the land
and enjoy great peace.

PSALM 37:11

PEACE LIKE A RIVER

ivers fascinate us. Each has its own special qualities: the speed of the current, the color of the water, the pattern of the ripples formed by the water curling around a rock or a log. Some rivers project a sense of excitement and power by their fast-moving currents; others peacefully and calmly meander along their way.

What is the "river of delights"? Look for clues about what is flowing in this river of delights in Psalm 36, verses 5-9: love, preservation, refuge, abundance, and life. God's love is boundless, reaching to the heaven, priceless and unfailing. God is offering you a drink—a taste of all that he desires to lavish on you.

God's river of delights is flowing out to you. God wants to satisfy your needs and your desires.

This is what the LORD says:

"I will extend peace to her like a river,
    and the wealth of nations like a flooding
stream. ...
As a mother comforts her child,
    so will I comfort you."

ISAIAH 66:12–13

One day Jesus and his friends set sail across the Sea of Galilee to relax. Suddenly, without warning, the winds changed and big waves began breaking over the boat, filling it with water. Frightened, the disciples went to Jesus, who was asleep in the back of the boat.

They woke him up and demanded to know, "Teacher, don't you care if we drown?" Jesus was cool. He turned to the elements and said, "Quiet! Be still!"

Then he turned back to his disciples and asked two poignant questions: "Why are you so afraid?" And, "Do you still have no faith?" (Mark 4:37-40).

The disciples didn't get it. Even though they had been with Jesus when he had changed the water to wine, healed the sick, gave sight to the blind, and opened deaf ears, here they were allowing the wind and big waves to frighten them, even though the Savior was with them.

Evidence of God's presence and power is all around us in the universe—the sun, the stars, the birth of each new day.

When stormy weather rolls in around you, cry out to Jesus. Listen to his still small voice as he whispers to you, "Why are you so afraid? Do you still have no faith?" When the gale is raging, you can be assured that he is standing by, speaking peace to your soul.

Thelma Wells

MEDITATIONS ON
PEACE LIKE A RIVER

*"I will extend peace to her like a river,
    and the wealth of nations like a flooding stream,"
        declares the LORD.*

ISAIAH 66:12

*The LORD leads me beside quiet waters,
    he restores my soul.*

PSALM 23:2–3

*The apostle John wrote about heaven, "The angel
showed me the river of the water of life, as clear
as crystal, flowing from the throne of God and of
the Lamb down the middle of the great street of
the city. On each side of the river stood the tree of
life, bearing twelve crops of fruit, yielding its
fruit every month. And the leaves of the tree are
for the healing of the nations. No longer will
there be any curse.*

*The throne of God and of the Lamb will be in the
city, and his servants will serve him. They will see
his face, and his name will be on their foreheads.
There will be no more night. They will not need
the light of a lamp or the light of the sun, for the
Lord God will give them light. And they will
reign for ever and ever."*

REVELATION 22:1–5

THE LORD'S PEACE

*C*ircumstances today are far from rosy. The world finds itself in chaos. Many a family is in a crisis. The church is often at a loss for the right answers. Small wonder that our hearts lack peace and are full of uncertainty. But in spite of this we can experience the Lord's peace continually, and in every way.

Peace must be practical and practiced! We best begin each new day with God, reading his Word and praying. Then we can think back to this quiet time throughout the day to claim his peace when unrest and discord are knocking at our door. We must remind ourselves that no situation we find ourselves in is beyond the range of God's interest in us.

Gien Karssen

*W*hen you're afraid, do as David did when he confronted Goliath. He says, "When I am afraid, I will trust in God". Fear is an opportunity to expand your faith in God. It is an opportunity to run to the Lord as your shelter. You can find refuge "under his wings" Bring your fears, anxieties and concerns to God, the only One who is fully able to calm your storms and defeat your Goliaths.

THE *Peace* OF GOD

*I*n a world filled with strife, peace often seems too elusive to even hope for. But Scripture makes it clear that peace is indeed possible. God is a God of peace, and peace comes from him.

Peace will come when you embrace the presence of God in your life. Jesus is the Prince of Peace. He has promised to meet your needs, shelter you, and rescue you. If you have no peace, perhaps you have taken your eyes off Jesus. Trust him. He is always with you. In the midst of turmoil, do your best to turn your eyes to him. "And the peace of God, which transcends all understanding, will guard your hearts and your minds in Christ Jesus" (Philippians 4:7).

*T*he struggles and tragedies of this life need not affect your joy as a Child of God. True joy is based on the spiritual realities of who God is and what he has promised. God *is* good and God *is* faithful—regardless of your situation.

You have no need to fear or to be anxious. Despite your circumstances you can "glory in his holy name", and your heart can rejoice as you seek him and the strength he offers.

MEDITATIONS ON
THE LORD'S PEACE

God is not a God of disorder but of peace.

1 CORINTHIANS 14:33

LORD, you establish peace for us.

ISAIAH 26:12

"I will heal my people and will let them enjoy abundant peace and security," declares the LORD.

JEREMIAH 33:6

*You will keep in perfect peace
    him whose mind is steadfast,
    because he trusts in you, O LORD.*

ISAIAH 26:3

COMFORT IN THE NIGHT

*G*race to you and peace from God our
Father and the Lord Jesus Christ.

PHILEMON 1:3

In some of the darkest hours of his life, van
Gogh found a single, graceful flower, and he
made that his focus. His outside world at the
asylum was grim at best, and everything around
him was a reminder of his internal sadness. Yet
somehow van Gogh, when he saw the irises, was
able to connect himself to the only lovely thing
in his surroundings. Captured by the flowers'
gracefulness, he painted them several times.

I, too, have seen grace in God's creations—
a swan gliding across a still pond, a gazelle
leaping across an African plain, an eagle
soaring above a craggy cliff. As effortless as
those movements are, so is the ease with which
God bestows his extravagant gift of grace into
our lives.

Grace is stunning. It is breathtaking. It is more
beautiful than van Gogh's Irises. Grace finds
us in our poverty and presents us with the gift
of an inheritance we didn't deserve ... the gift
of grace.

Patsy Clairmont

His Everlasting Arms

I cried,
Lord, I'm so afraid tonight.
There's no rest for my soul.
Besieged by worry, fear, and pain,
I tossed and turned and rolled.
I prayed,
Lord, send your angel,
Someone to hold my hand,
Someone to touch my broken heart
And say, "I understand."
I prayed,
Lord, send a candle
To light this long, dark night,
A flame to warm and cheer me,
To set my soul aright.
I prayed,
Lord, send ...
Then, that was all.
For what He sent to me
Was peace.
His everlasting arms
Carried me off
To sleep.

Ann Luna

MEDITATIONS ON
COMFORT IN THE NIGHT

*Praise be to the God and Father of our Lord
Jesus Christ, the Father of compassion and
the God of all comfort, who comforts us in all
our troubles.*

2 CORINTHIANS 1:3–4

*Even though I walk
    through the valley of the shadow of death,
I will fear no evil,
    for you are with me, O LORD;
your rod and your staff,
    they comfort me.*

PSALM 23:4

*"As a mother comforts her Child,
    so will I comfort you,"
        declares the Lord.*

ISAIAH 66:13

ACCEPTING GOD'S PLAN

*A*my Carmichael says, "In acceptance lieth peace." Solomon advises us to accept what God has given us as a gift: "To enjoy your work and to accept your lot in life—that is indeed a gift from God". (Ecclesiastes 5:19 LB).

During the years I worked for Mobil Oil Corporation, there were numerous times I wanted to leave. Quit. Give it up and find a job that had more personal or spiritual gratification. But I believed God had put me in that environment for a purpose.

Finally, after many years, I accepted the fact that God wanted me to work for Mobil and to stay until he moved me for his own good reasons. Peace came to me when I stopped fighting.

I stayed with Mobil for thirty years, and I have never regretted it. The financial savings I started there grew to a next egg that enables me to have a very comfortable retirement. The professional growth and experience of those years have helped me in decision making, goal setting, and general maturing. And friends? To this day, those with whom I worked are among the most precious ones in my life.

Luci Swindoll

*J*oy is not only an emotion to be desired, it is also a command to be obeyed. Joy is—to some degree—a choice. How can this be? Are you to simply ignore your circumstances and live outside of reality" No, but a life of joy can be learned—and suffering is most often the teacher.

The Scriptures clearly point out the path toward a life of joy: accept your circumstances and be thankful in them, choose not to worry, fix your eyes on Jesus rather than on your situation—follow his example in suffering—and put your hope in future glory. It is through the joy and peace exhibited in suffering that God is most visible in your life. When you live a life of joy—regardless of your circumstances—others will see Jesus in you.

Whatever your current circumstances, God longs to comfort you, heal you and give you his peace, joy and hope. Take your needs to him in prayer. Lay all your hurts and worries before him. Ask him to help you accept your circumstances, fix your eyes on Jesus and live life in joy and peace.

MEDITATIONS ON ACCEPTING GOD'S PLAN

"I know the plans I have for you," declares the LORD, "plans to prosper you and not to harm you, plans to give you hope and a future."

JEREMIAH 29:11

Our Father in heaven,
hallowed be your name,
*   your kingdom come,*
your will be done
*   on earth as it is in heaven.*

MATTHEW 6:9–10

Do not conform any longer to the pattern of this world, but be transformed by the renewing of your mind. Then you will be able to test and approve what God's will is—his good, pleasing and perfect will.

ROMANS 12:2

TRUST IN THE LORD

*G*od uses circumstances, things and people to test you. When you face trials and testing, you have a choice. You can choose to trust the strength of the Lord, or you can choose to rely on yourself. Depending on yourself results in corruption and deception. Depending on God results in the
ability to rejoice regardless of the circumstances.

If you are enduring testing, be aware of the clear choices before you. If you trust in worldly power, wealth, friends or family, neighbors, or your own understanding, you will be disappointed. But "the LORD is good, a refuge in times of trouble. He cares for those who trust in him". Trust him, and be filled with joy, peace and hope.

To the precise extent that we trust Him, we are enabled to live in His peace without fear for today or apprehension for the future.

Emily Gardiner Neal, quoted by Sue Buchanan

Trust in the LORD with all your heart
 and lean not on your own understanding;
in all your ways acknowledge him,
 and he will make your paths straight.

PROVERBS 3:5–6

*D*oes God ever seem too far away, too fearsome, too holy? How can this kind of God be a comfort to you? You know in your mind that God can be trusted, yet your heart resists.

A person's natural inclination is to want to know what's ahead. Trusting God does not mean he will tell you what's going to happen. It means you know you are safe with him—no matter what happens. You can take on the adventures God has planned because you know he is there to protect you. You can meet your troubles head-on because you know God will provide for you. Trust allows you to accept and appreciate all the surprises of life.

God speaks to us clearly. He means what he says. When he says he'll provide, we can count on that. When he promises peace, wisdom, strength, or comfort, they are ours. God imparts his word and keeps it.

Luci Swindoll

*T*hrough actively walking with God, we are conformed to His will; and as we walk, our faith to follow Him increases. By freely responding to the grace of obedience with our whole hearts, we enter a new realm of trust in God.

Debra Evans

MEDITATIONS ON
TRUSTING IN THE LORD

Trust in the LORD and do good;
dwell in the land and enjoy safe pasture.
Delight yourself in the LORD
and he will give you the desires of your heart.

Commit your way to the LORD;
trust in him and he will do this:
He will make your righteousness shine like
the dawn,
the justice of your cause like the noonday sun.

PSALM 37:3–6

We wait in hope for the LORD;
he is our help and our shield.
In him our hearts rejoice,
for we trust in his holy name.
May your unfailing love rest upon us, O
LORD,
even as we put our hope in you.

PSALM 33:20–22

HONESTY WITH GOD

*D*avid spoke the truth to God. He poured out his pain and his questions. He agonized over the sin that cast a dark cloud over his soul. Yet, in the midst of his darkest moments, there are gifts of grace ... pearls of peace.

David spoke the truth. He faced his fears head-on, and following that authentic path led him to receive the gift of peace. I believe that deep, abiding peace is possible only when all our cards are on the table before the Lord. I'm convinced we can't be at peace if we are attempting to hide our true selves from God. Facing our deepest fears means making peace with our *seen self* and with our *unseen self*. We all have both.

I am learning to bring *all* the parts of me into God's presence, into the circle of his embrace, because I have become convinced that this is the only path to peace.

Sheila Walsh

*M*y dear friend, Ney Bailey, encourages me to let my current anxieties be the springboard for praying specifically. In other words, when I'm worried about something, have financial troubles or relationship problems— whatever—I let that troublesome thing be the catalyst for talking to God in straightforward detail. I don't skirt what's bugging me. I don't act like it doesn't exist. I don't go on to other things. Right in the middle of my anxiety, I tell God about it, as if he were my dad.

Ney also told me not to edit me prayers. I absolutely love that thought! When a child pulls at his mother's coattail for something he wants, he doesn't stand there thinking, *Now, how should I phrase this ... let's see. Shall I start with "I want," or is that too forward?* Goodness, no! The kid blurts out his thoughts spontaneously, with total abandon. The sincerity of his heart exposes his deepest desires. Praying to our heavenly Father this way fosters a bonding that's sweet and comforting.

Luci Swindoll

MEDITATIONS ON
HONESTY WITH GOD

*Let us draw near to God with a sincere heart
in full assurance of faith.*

HEBREWS 10:22

*Trust in the LORD at all times, O people;
    pour out your hearts to him,
    for God is our refuge.*

PSALM 62:8

*I know, my God, that you test the heart and
are pleased with integrity.*

1 CHRONICLES 29:17

*The righteous cry out, and the LORD hears them;
    he delivers them from all their troubles.
The LORD is close to the brokenhearted
    and saves those who are crushed in spirit.*

PSALM 34:17–18

*Let us ... approach the throne of grace with
confidence, so that we may receive mercy and
find grace to help us in our time of need.*

HEBREWS 4:16

GOD'S DELIGHT IN YOU

*I*magine hearing God sing. Does it sound like the mighty roar of thunder, or like a soft and gentle whisper? It is powerful and strong, yet unimaginably beautiful, pure and sweet. And, he is singing that glorious song over you! Why does God sing over you? Because he delights in you. *You* make his heart sing with joy.

God's love for you is deep and strong. It will never be shaken. You are secure in him. Knowing that he delights in you can give you freedom to delight in him and in all that he has for you.

Rejoice in knowing that God is glorified as you are spiritually transformed. When you take a step of faith, when you grow and mature, he is singing over you from a heart bursting with joy and pride. He is your loving Father. Listen to the special love song he is singing just for you.

*W*hat is so astounding to me it that God does not say, "As long as you don't stumble, Marilyn, I'll hang around and be supportive." Rather, he says he *delights* in every detail of my life. Not because the details are always delightful, but because he is my hand-holding God who walks with me through the events of my life no matter how foolish or misguided my steps may be. In fact, he uses those very experiences to deepen and strengthen my relationship with him. ·

The LORD delights in those who fear him,
who put their hope in his unfailing love.

PSALM 147:11

*H*ow blessed each of us is to have such a compassionate, faithful God! When we feel like we've made a mess of things (even if it's only by mistake), we can be sure that our ever-waiting Lord will not only remove the mess, but show us the fullness of his boundless love as we wait for rescue.

Marilyn Meberg

MEDITATIONS ON
GOD'S DELIGHT IN YOU

The LORD your God is with you,
he is mighty to save.
He will take great delight in you,
he will quiet you with his love,
he will rejoice over you with singing.

ZEPHANIAH 3:17

As a bridegroom rejoices over his bride,
so will your God rejoice over you.

ISAIAH 62:5

How great is the love the Father has lavished
on us, that we should be called children of
God! And that is what we are!

1 JOHN 3:1

The LORD appeared to us in the past, saying:

"I have loved you with an everlasting love;
I have drawn you with loving-kindness."

JEREMIAH 31:3

SEEING THROUGH
GOD'S EYES

*C*orrie ten Boom held up a piece of cloth to the crowd gathered before her and asked them what they saw. It wasn't very impressive. Threads ran in conflicting directions, and there was no clear picture or continuity to the piece. It was so knotted in places that it actually looked ugly. Then she turned it over. It was breathtaking. On the other side, the "right" side, was a beautiful crown embroidered in exquisite detail. What the audience had seen up until that point was only the mass of knotted threads on the back.

That's how I see things now. We're looking at our lives from the back, and all we can see are the knots where new thread was used and colors changed. What God sees is the other side. He sees what we are becoming—the beautiful picture he designed before the world began. What a hope! Not because any of us in our own strength could make anything even the dog would sit on, but because God is doing it. Right now, if all the knots of your life look ugly to you, take heart. God is making something you'll want to frame for eternity.

Sheila Walsh

THE *Peace* OF GOD

So much of our anxiety about the days to come fades when we look at our life through God's eternal perspective. That is why God reassures our troubled soul with the invitation to trust him—to have confidence about his good intentions for our life.

Valerie Bell

"My thoughts are not your thoughts,
neither are your ways my ways,"
declares the LORD.
"As the heavens are higher than the earth,
so are my ways higher than your ways
and my thoughts than your thoughts."

ISAIAH 55:8–9

Sometimes we go to the Lord asking for favors without understanding what we are really saying. We may feel crushed when he says no, but he only withholds out of love. He has the wisdom of all eternity at his disposal and is a wise judge. Ask him to reveal his perspective. It will make all the difference.

MEDITATIONS ON SEEING THROUGH GOD'S EYES

If you call out for insight
and cry aloud for understanding,
and if you look for it as for silver
and search for it as for hidden treasure,
then you will understand the fear of the LORD
and find the knowledge of God.
For the LORD gives wisdom,
and from his mouth come knowledge and
understanding.

PROVERBS 2:3–6

Blessed is the man who finds wisdom,
the man who gains understanding,
for she is more profitable than silver
and yields better returns than gold.
She is more precious than rubies;
nothing you desire can compare with her.
Long life is in her right hand;
in her left hand are riches and honor.
Her ways are pleasant ways,
and all her paths are peace.

PROVERBS 3:13–17

NOTHING IS PERMANENT

I have this wonderful doctor, and some years back I was talking to him about a mutual friend of ours who'd had a face-lift. "Face-lifts are fine," he said, "but they only last for about five years. Nothing is permanent."

"Nothing is permanent." I chewed on that. *True, I thought. Nothing this side of heaven is absolute. Nothing is forever. Hair will be shorn; hair will grow back (usually). Faces will fall, no matter how many times we get them lifted. The future is unknown. Times change, we change, everything changes. Except the taste of postage-stamp glue.*

Just as I was starting to *really* depress myself, another bottom-line truth came into my mind: "I the LORD do not change. So you, O descendants of Jacob, are not destroyed" (Malachi 3:6). Whew! Nothing remains the same (you don't even have to lick postage stamps anymore) … *except God.* God's character is immutable and his Word is final. His stubborn love for us never varies or wavers. Regardless of our behavior, our losses, or the droop of our face, God's promises are true, and his love holds us fast.

Barbara Johnson

*W*hat a good thing it is that God created us with a built-in ability to change.

The unhappy people are the ones who feel threatened by the changes going on around them. They look to traditions and institutions to give them a sense of security. Newness frightens them. They become rigid and in their presence there is no peace.

But there are others who haven't hardened. Feeling the flow of life, they move in rhythm with it. Their trust in Christ is so real, and the security he gives them is so strong, that they cannot be threatened by change. They realize that newness is inherent in life … that if they themselves are going to expand and grow, they too must change. But they aren't dominated by change—they are free to evaluate it, to reject or accept it, according to its merits. These are the meek people of the world, and when I am with them I sense peace. With God's help, I want to be more like them.

Colleen Townsend Evans

MEDITATIONS ON PEACE IN TIMES OF CHANGE

God does not change like shifting shadows.

JAMES 1:17

Your word, O LORD, is eternal;
it stands firm in the heavens.
Your faithfulness continues through all
generations.

PSALM 119:89–90

God rides on the heavens to help you
and on the clouds in his majesty.
The eternal God is your refuge,
and underneath are the everlasting arms.

DEUTERONOMY 33:26–27

"Though the mountains be shaken
and the hills be removed,
yet my unfailing love for you will not be shaken
nor my covenant of peace be removed,"
says the LORD, who has compassion on you.

ISAIAH 54:10

GOD'S INVOLVEMENT
IN YOUR LIFE

One evening, as Ney and I were enjoying a late dinner, I once again shared with her what has been a spiritual conundrum to me most of my adult life: to what degree is God active in the minutia of daily living? I wobble back and forth on this issue. Of course I can and do talk to him about everything; that's part of maintaining my spiritual connection. And of course I know he loves me and cares about all facets of my experience. But tennis tickets … do I really take *that* request to him? It almost seems like magical thinking to pray for tickets, and when we get them, assume God brought it about.

As Ney and I tossed this subject around, she said something, as she has so many times in our twenty-two-year friendship, that made me suddenly very quiet at the center of my soul: "I learned years ago not to edit my prayers." She explained that her job is to "make her requests known," as child would, and then, no matter the result, trust that God is praised and honored. "Like a father, it pleases him to give good gifts to his children," Ney said. "And Marilyn, God gifted both of us with a great day of tennis! Our job is simply to unwrap his gracious gift … and enjoy!"

Marilyn Meberg

*O*ur God is sovereign. There is nothing too big, too small, too imminent or too distant to escape his notice and control. Sometimes events in life that seem catastrophic at the moment can be seen in retrospect as blessings from God. When we suffer such seeming setbacks, then is the time our faith in him must be strongest, whether or not we ever understand his reasons.

O Sovereign LORD, you have begun to show to your servant your greatness and your strong hand. For what god is there in heaven or on earth who can do the deeds and mighty works you do?

DEUTERONOMY 3:24

Ah, Sovereign LORD, you have made the heavens and the earth by your great power and out-stretched arm. Nothing is too hard for you.

JEREMIAH 32:17

Meditations on God's Involvement in Your Life

Cast all your anxiety on him because he cares for you.

1 Peter 5:7

In everything, by prayer and petition, with thanksgiving, present your requests to God.

Philippians 4:6

Pray in the Spirit on all occasions with all kinds of prayers and requests.

Ephesians 6:18

Be joyful always; pray continually; give thanks in all circumstances, for this is God's will for you in Christ Jesus.

1 Thessalonians 5:16–18

The eyes of the Lord are on the righteous and his ears are attentive to their prayer.

1 Peter 3:12

HE WHO WATCHES
OVER YOU

*M*y night-light brings back memories of
lying in bed at night as a little girl. I
remember cars turning the corner in front of our
house, their headlights momentarily invading
the darkness of my bedroom, against the door,
then the wall, the ceiling, and ultimately my
bed, in one long shaft of moving light. That light
made me feel safe, as if God were in the yard,
checking on me with his flashlight, just to let me
know he was around and everything was okay.

Luci Swindoll

*W*hen the circumstances of life over-
whelm, when we feel like we've been
treated unfairly, we can be sure that we serve a
"God who sees." He knows our circumstances,
and he sees what others have done to us. Just as
he watched over Hagar, he watches over us, with
compassion and a plan for our future (Genesis
16:6–13). He is not only a God who sees, he is
a God who acts and a God who can be trusted.

I can't begin to answer the question of why God does what he does in ways that I consider a bit off-kilter and odd, but I can certainly describe the lessons I learn from these methods. These lessons contribute a tremendous peace and soul satisfaction when fully understood. My peace is bolstered when I contemplate as well as experience God's totally unfathomable workings in my life. That's because I know for a fact that he's around! There's no other explanation for how things are going ... or not going. Sometimes his odd workings get my attention to the point of whiplashing me into a neck brace! My response is always "who but God?". When I have a "who but God?" reaction, I know who to credit for whatever is going on in my life—and that assurance produces peace.

Every now and then, I need to be reminded of who takes care of me and who is in charge of all the events in my life. When I'm skipping blithely across the high wire, or congratulating myself on my confidence and skill, it's easy to forget who my safety net is. Fortunately, God doesn't let me be the star of the show from start to finish. Sometimes he turns things completely upside down so that what is happening does not make sense to me at all! In fact, I lose my balance completely, and I'm forced to cling to him and rest in his peace that passes understanding.

Marilyn Meberg

MEDITATIONS ON GOD'S WATCHFULNESS

I lift up my eyes to the hills—
    where does my help come from?
My help comes from the LORD,
    the Maker of heaven and earth.

He will not let your foot slip—
    he who watches over you will not slumber;
indeed, he who watches over Israel
    will neither slumber nor sleep.

The LORD watches over you—
    the LORD is your shade at your right hand;
the sun will not harm you by day,
    nor the moon by night.

The LORD will keep you from all harm—
    he will watch over your life;
the LORD will watch over your coming and going
    both now and forevermore.

PSALM 121

GOD IS FAITHFUL

*I*n his first letter to the Corinthians, the apostle Paul reminds the early believers that they have abundant grace and peace from God the Father and the Lord Jesus Christ. "In him you have been enriched in every way," Paul says. "Therefore you do not lack any spiritual gift as you eagerly wait for our Lord Jesus Christ to be revealed. He will keep you strong to the end, so that you will be blameless on the day of our Lord Jesus Christ. God, who has called you into fellowship with his Son Jesus Christ our Lord, is faithful" (1 Corinthians 1:5, 7–9).

Each one of us is given everything spiritually that we need to remain "strong to the end." In the spiritual realm—the one beyond our physical sight, where God is busy initiating and completing divine activity—all is well. Even when there is chaos in our lives, we can experience indescribable peace because we know that whatever we are going through, God already knows about it and has equipped us to handle it with his grace. It is his faithfulness that gives us confidence and peace.

Thelma Wells

*D*uring my year of chemotherapy, when I wasn't sure whether I would die, it became important for me to sort myth from truth in regard to my personal faith. I came to see that God wasn't nearly as complicated as I had once thought Him to be—that other than keeping the Ten Commandments, there weren't a lot of rules. In fact, it became easy for me to think of God as a loving parent who sees the big picture, just as Wayne and I saw the big picture for our children when they were young and immature. I discovered that God was as close as I allowed Him to be. I could actually feel His presence.

After realizing that God was *there* and that He wasn't as complicated as I'd thought, the next thing I discovered was that there are answers to life's dilemmas in Holy Scripture. Sometimes we aren't even aware they are there until we need them. I was a tape recorder that could be turned on and off; push my button and I could turn on the verse that speaks of "… the peace of God, which transcends all understanding" (Philippians 4:7).

Sue Buchanan

MEDITATIONS ON GOD'S FAITHFULNESS

Because of the LORD'S great love we are not consumed,
*   for his compassions never fail.*
They are new every morning;
*   great is your faithfulness, O LORD.*

LAMENTATIONS 3:22–23

Your love, O LORD, reaches to the heavens,
*   your faithfulness to the skies.*
Your righteousness is like the mighty mountains,
*   your justice like the great deep.*

PSALM 36:5–6

He is the faithful God, keeping his covenant
of love to a thousand generations of those
who love him and keep his commands.

DEUTERONOMY 7:9

The word of the LORD is right and true;
*   he is faithful in all he does.*

PSALM 33:4

BASKETS OF BLESSINGS

*I*n her book *Basket of Blessings: 31 Days to a More Grateful Heart,* Karen O'Connor shares her experience with practicing thankfulness. "If you want to be content, to experience peace," a friend had told Karen, "write down your blessings—the things you're grateful for—on slips of paper and put them in a small basket or box or bag. Soon it will be full to overflowing. From time to time look at what you wrote. No one can be discontent for long with so much to be thankful for."

In addition to filling a "blessing basket" on a daily basis, we could write a letter to God once a year, listing all that pours out of our hearts for his extravagant grace to us. Think of what a joy it would be to keep our annual letters of gratitude to read through the years or to pass on to our children.

Whether our "thank you's" are momentary, intentional pauses in the midst of a hectic day, thank-you notes to God for his many blessings, or lengthy discourses of his grace, cultivating an attitude of gratitude will remind us of the truth that undergirds our lives: "For the Lord is good and his love endures forever; his faithfulness continues through all generations" (Psalm 100:5).

Sheila Walsh 47

I love that a day has boundaries so I can measure it. From sunrise to sunset, from morning to evening, from a sunlit day to a starlit night, hours collect into a lifetime. As I reflect on my collection, I'm reminded what a gift life is and, how precious each twenty-four-hour increment is. I also realize that the days I thought would never end are some of the sweeter memories that I hold up now like a multi-faceted diamond refracting light.

One of those sparkling facets is God's extravagant grace, which has been so clearly extended to me throughout my life's journey. He helped me to take the next step on the good days and on the bad—especially the bad.

Dear friend, embrace your day—this day—it is a gift. Take the Lord's hand. He will help you to unwrap the day and then to celebrate it. And his grace will be sufficient for any need you have.

Patsy Clairmont

MEDITATIONS ON CELEBRATING GOD'S GIFTS

This is the day the LORD has made;
let us rejoice and be glad in it.

PSALM 118:24

Every good and perfect gift is from above,
coming down from the Father of the heavenly
lights.

JAMES 1:17

Give thanks to the LORD, for he is good;
his love endures forever.

PSALM 118:29

The apostle Paul wrote, "I have learned the
secret of being content in any and every situ-
ation, whether well fed or hungry, whether
living in plenty or in want. I can do every-
thing through him who gives me strength."

PHILIPPIANS 4:12–13

Our True Soul Mate

*A*ging has given me an appreciation for things that are not trendy but classic. Classic-cut jeans and suits appeal. I love the patina of my wood antiques; they just get better with age. I collect American pottery because I know it is timeless—as beautiful one hundred years from now as it was the day it was created.

When it comes to my soul, I am experiencing the same directional desire. I want classic, tried-and-true intimacy with God. I do not want just human connectedness, however global. I want to experience my Soul Mate. I do not want to settle for being in tune with nature and ancestors. Yes, I am interested in depth and tired of superficiality. But I realize any version of deeper life, apart from God, will not satisfy. My soul was created to be a God-fit. I am incomplete without him, frustrated and dissatisfied with other substitutes. God is the goal of soul; all other hungers are symptomatic of the soul's longing to connect to its soul mate—God.

Valerie Bell

*D*oes the idea of intimacy with God frighten you? "Who could be intimate with a holy, righteous God?" you ask. Yes, God is holy and righteous, and he is also loving and compassionate. God reveals himself in Scripture as a father and as a husband. He provides for you and protects you as a loving father. As your husband he desires to meet your need for intimacy.

God says that Israel "will call me 'my husband'". These are the words of a lover—God—in pursuit of his beloved—Israel. God is in pursuit of you, too. He wants an intimate relationship with you—one that will last forever, one that will satisfy your deepest needs. You can respond to God by allowing him to draw you into his loving arms. Your life, your relationships, your reactions—all will be affected by God's embrace.

If you desire intimacy with God, go to him in prayer. He is waiting. He will rejoice, and he will treat you with tenderness and compassion. He is the perfect lover of your soul, one who will never disappoint, one who will be faithful, true and loving.

MEDITATIONS ON
OUR TRUE SOUL MATE

I delight greatly in the LORD;
my soul rejoices in my God.
For he has clothed me with garments of salvation
and arrayed me in a robe of righteousness,
as a bridegroom adorns his head like a priest,
and as a bride adorns herself with her jewels.

ISAIAH 61:10

"I am the LORD, your God,
the Holy One of Israel, your Savior ...
You are precious and honored in my sight,
and ... I love you."

ISAIAH 43:3–4

Hallelujah!
For our Lord God Almighty reigns.
Let us rejoice and be glad
and give him glory
For the wedding of the Lamb has come,
and his bride has made herself ready.
Fine linen, bright and clean,
was given her to wear.

REVELATION 19:6–8

NOAH WALKED WITH GOD

*D*o we stay in this job or accept another offer? Do we join the big Church on the corner or the newly formed storefront congregation? Should we enroll our kids in public school or private? How do we decide which choice God wants us to make? The Bible says Noah "walked with God". It doesn't say he *talked* with God. Instead the image implies quiet companionship. Noah walked with God—and, no doubt, he listened. He "found favor in the eyes of the Lord".

Noah spent time with the Father, and during their time together God spoke to him. And as outrageous as God's instructions may have seemed at the time, Noah set about building an ark. He stepped out with courage to do what he perceived as God's will. And later, if Noah had learned that God had been telling him to build a "park" instead of an "ark," he would have asked forgiveness and started over. For Noah served the same God we serve, a great God of grace.

Barbara Johnson

*I*magine you are planning to build a new home. First you go to a good architect— one you trust to draw up a good plan. Next you find qualified builders to do the construction and artisans to finish the work. After the building is completed, you furnish it with your personal treasures to make your house your home.

Each day you are in the process of building a spiritual house. What determines your plans and influences your decisions? Is your life built on a solid foundation, or have you haphazardly thrown pieces of construction material together? It's never too late to do some remodeling.

Make wisdom the basis for all that is planned, built and done in your life. Do you feel incapable of building anything of value? You can ask the master builder and architect of the universe to help you.

God delights in giving wisdom. When you seek it, you will find it, and it "will enter your heart, and knowledge will be pleasant to your soul. Discretion will protect you, and understanding will guard you" (Proverbs 2:10–11). What beautiful promises!

MEDITATIONS ON GOD'S WISDOM AND GUIDANCE

*In your unfailing love you will lead
    the people you have redeemed, O LORD.
In your strength you will guide them.*

EXODUS 15:13

*I guide you in the way of wisdom
    and lead you along straight paths.
When you walk, your steps will not be hampered;
    when you run, you will not stumble.*

PROVERBS 4:11–12

*The LORD will guide you always;
    he will satisfy your needs in a sun-
scorched land
    and will strengthen your frame.
You will be like a well-watered garden,
    like a spring whose waters never fail.*

ISAIAH 58:11

OUR CORE IDENTITY

*G*od does not define us by our roles or by our relationships. He knows us by our hearts, our character, our intrinsic eternal selves. Our souls are what identify us to God. We look to our labels; God looks to our core. Labels like child of … , mother of … , wife of …. , Christian broadcaster, author, singer, beautiful woman, teacher, businesswoman, or psychiatric patient, only describe where we have been—not who we are!

We can lose many identities in life, but in the end, our souls remain. We are so much more than our labels. We are more than our health; we are more than our beauty or our life's achievements. We are more than any defining relationship or our mental health. We are more than our image or what we are perceived to be. We can lose every drop of perceived specialness and still, soul—that deep, intrinsic, individual identifying specialness—remains.

God remains as well. Nothing can change that. A shift to internal values away from external perceptions is sustaining. A woman who cares more for her soul than she does about the labels she has acquired, who is focused on the work of becoming God's friend, has an abiding, immutable center.

Valerie Bell

*W*e frequently feel pulled in a dozen different directions, pressured by contemporary role models who encourage us to look at a job or our looks as the central core of our identity—when our greatest joy and highest privilege as believers is designed to come from knowing, serving, and loving our Lord.

As we seek to serve our Savior and humbly live according to his unduplicatable design for our lives, we see that our self-worth is based on God's view of us, not on our own opinions or others' attitudes toward us. Our identity becomes securely centered in the reality of what Jesus has accomplished on our behalf, not on what we have accomplished for ourselves.

Proclaiming the Lord's love often requires a sacrifice of our personal ease. It takes courage, time and effort. As the following verse from the old Celtic hymn "Be Thou My Vision" explains, it takes an ardent desire to view creation with the eyes of Christ:

> *Be Thou my vision, O Lord of my heart,*
> *Naught be all else to me save that Thou art—*
> *Thou my best thought, by day or by night,*
> *Waking or sleeping, Thy presence my light.*

Deborah Evans

MEDITATIONS ON
OUR CORE IDENTITY

*The LORD does not look at the things
man looks at. Man looks at the outward
appearance, but the LORD looks at the heart.*

1 SAMUEL 16:7

You created my inmost being, O LORD;
    you knit me together in my mother's womb.
*I praise you because I am fearfully and
wonderfully made;*
    your works are wonderful,
    I know that full well.
My frame was not hidden from you
    when I was made in the secret place.
*When I was woven together in the depths of
the earth,*
    your eyes saw my unformed body.
All the days ordained for me
    were written in your book
    before one of them came to be.

PSALM 139:13–16

MEDITATIONS ON
OUR CORE IDENTITY

*"Why spend money on what is not bread,
      and your labor on what does not satisfy?
Listen, listen to me, and eat what is good,
      and your soul will delight in the richest
of fare.
Give ear and come to me;
      hear me, that your soul may live."
            declares the Lord.*

ISAIAH 55:2–3

*Great is the Lord and mighty in power;
      his understanding has no limit.*

PSALM 147:5

*Find rest, O my soul, in God alone;
      my hope comes from him.
He alone is my rock and my salvation;
      he is my fortress, I will not be shaken.
My salvation and my honor depend on God;
      he is my mighty rock, my refuge.*

PSALM 62:5–7

GOD UNDERSTANDS US

*S*ometimes I come to God distracted,
offering only my presence and little else.
Though I long for deep connectedness, I thwart
my own desires by trying to give him just my
mind (what I think as opposed to what I feel).
But God wants all of me. I can be vulnerable
with God. There is great comfort in such intimacy. One of my friends who has suffered a
great deal in life calls God "the God of Extreme
Understanding." I like that name for God. That
is the God I have met when I come naked-
souled to him. The God of Extreme Understanding. We cannot be too honest or too open or too
hurting or too sad to turn God away from
embracing our souls.

Valerie Bell

We are often reluctant to share our deepest feelings with the Lord. Irrationally, we believe if we don't say it, he won't know it. The Lord wants us to be totally honest and open with him. He can surely handle our strongest emotions. As we confess our struggles, we lay down our pride and learn from his counsel.

No matter what our age, we all long to be accepted, but so many times we are not. Perhaps that's why we become so defensive, why we allow ourselves to be angry or look tough rather than to feel fear. One thing I do know to be true: we will never be rejected by God. He will never be too busy for us or annoyed by us. He will never call us names or make us feel small in a way that destroys our dignity.

I learn a lot through my little son. When he is hurt, he cries. He tells me what made him sad, and he allows himself to be comforted. God is there for us with open arms if we will be honest enough to present ourselves needy and hurt. He will hear our every cry. He will comfort us, dust us off, kiss away our tears, and send us back— fearless—to the playground of our lives.

Sheila Walsh

MEDITATIONS ON GOD'S UNDERSTANDING

O LORD, you have searched me
*   and you know me.*
You know when I sit and when I rise;
*   you perceive my thoughts from afar.*
You discern my going out and my lying down;
*   you are familiar with all my ways.*
Before a word is on my tongue
*   you know it completely, O LORD.*

You hem me in—behind and before;
*   you have laid your hand upon me.*
Such knowledge is too wonderful for me,
*   too lofty for me to attain.*

Where can I go from your Spirit?
*   Where can I flee from your presence?*
If I go up to the heavens, you are there;
*   if I make my bed in the depths, you are there.*
If I rise on the wings of the dawn,
*   if I settle on the far side of the sea,*
even there your hand will guide me,
*   your right hand will hold me fast.*

PSALM 139:1–10

GOD'S PURPOSE FOR YOU

*W*hat is your dream? What do you deeply desire? Could it be that those desires have been planted in your heart by the heavenly Father? Do you believe he has a purpose for your most cherished dream because it originated with him? God wants you to pursue the talents he has created within you. He means for them to blossom through your personality. Your availability makes it happen.

Each one of us has ideas spinning in her heart and head. They are there for a reason. If we allow our desires to be purified by the Holy Spirit, fueled by the light of Christ, and warmed by our passion for God's will, we will make a difference in this world.

Barbara Johnson

*T*here are times when, oh, what we wouldn't give for a little direction. Desperately we long for God's guidance. How many times have I heard people say, "I really want to do what God wants me to do, but what is it? What is his will anyway?"

Consider this as a rule of thumb: God never calls without enabling us. In other words, if he calls you to do something, he makes it possible for you to do it.

Luci Swindoll

*W*hen we realize our days here matter, our pain has significance, and our choices are meaningful, we can step through the darkest of times with hope in our hearts. It's not that we won't waver, but even our inquiries have the potential, when we are seeking, to lead us to a stronger faith.

I find that my joy is enlarged by understanding that, as child of God, even my pain has purpose. That realization doesn't eliminate my pain, but it makes it more manageable.

Patsy Clairmont

*S*top and listen to God every day, quiet your spirit before him, ask him to communicate with you. God has plenty to say to you, but he requires your undivided attention. Psalm 46 verse 10 tells us that we will *know God* and his sovereignty when we are "still." Be still and know his will for you today.

Thelma Wells

MEDITATIONS ON GOD'S PURPOSE FOR YOU

"Be still, and know that I am God.
I will be exalted among the nations,
I will be exalted in the earth," says the LORD.

PSALM 46:10

It is God who works in you to will and to act
according to his good purpose.

PHILIPPIANS 2:13

I desire to do your will, O my God;
your law is within my heart.

PSALM 40:8

We are God's workmanship, created in Christ
Jesus to do good works, which God prepared
in advance for us to do.

EPHESIANS 2:10

The LORD will fulfill his purpose for me;
your love, O LORD, endures forever.

PSALM 138:8

GOD'S EXTRAVAGANT LOVE

*I*f you are like me, you often feel like two people. Some days we live in such a way that our actions cry out praise to God. On other days it's as if we crucify Christ all over again.

The most wonderful thing about the love of God expressed in Christ is that none of this is a surprise to him. God entrusted his Son to a harsh, cruel world knowing that it would first embrace him and then spit on him and kill him. And yet he did it anyway—because his love has no limits. God's love cannot be quenched by the ever-turning tides of human emotion and devotion.

God knows all about you. He knows your good days and your bad days. He knows the noble thoughts and the shameful thoughts. He sees your devotion and your indifference. And he loves you—totally, completely, passionately, boundlessly. Forever.

Sheila Walsh

*G*et yourself a cup of tea, curl up in your favorite chair, and read this wonderful story [Song of Songs] about the love of one girl and one king and how their love illustrates God's boundless, fearless, stubborn, lavish, outlandish, intentional love for you. God's love is sweeter than honey dripping from a honeycomb, more beautiful than the first flowers in spring, cozier than a warm blanket on a winter night, peaceful as the gentlest breeze, vast as the full moon surrounded by the endless galaxies, comfortable as a good night's rest.

Thelma Wells

*G*od loves us because of who he is ... it is his nature. His love is not measured out to us in carefully leveled teaspoons corresponding to our responsiveness or lack of response, our attractiveness or our repulsiveness—it is not doled out to us according to what we deserve. Instead, he lavishes—mounds, heaps, piles on—his love, like a sundae over-dipped with sweet chocolate syrup running over the sides, over the tabletop, down the sides, and onto the floor.

Valerie Bell

MEDITATIONS ON GOD'S EXTRAVAGANT LOVE

Great is your love, O LORD, reaching to the heavens;
>	*your faithfulness reaches to the skies.*

PSALM 57:10

Because your love is better than life,
>	*my lips will glorify you.*
I will praise you as long as I live, O LORD,
>	*and in your name I will lift up my hands.*
My soul will be satisfied as with the richest of foods;
>	*with singing lips my mouth will praise you.*

PSALM 63:3–5

I will sing of the LORD'S great love forever;
>	*with my mouth I will make your faithfulness known through all generations.*
I will declare that your love stands firm forever,
>	*that you established your faithfulness in heaven itself.*

PSALM 89:1–2

GOD'S WORD:
A LIGHT FOR MY PATH

*O*ne of the featured art pieces at the J. Paul Getty Museum in Los Angeles is *Prayerbook for a Queen: The Hours of Jeanne d'Evreux*. This tiny, artistic masterpiece was a gift to the queen of France seven hundred years ago.

As I considered the queen's book, I couldn't help thinking about the King's book, the Bible. Now there is a journal if I ever saw one. Talk about exquisite; have you read David's psalms lately? Open up to a page and read afresh the sweet songs of a young shepherd, hear the cries of a pursued warrior, and the anguish of a repentant king.

Talk about art, the Song of Solomon, the book of Ruth, and the creation account paint vivid pictures on the canvas of our hearts. Each word from the Scriptures, like brush-strokes, allows us breathtaking views all the way from Mount Nebo, to the crystal river flowing from God's throne.

No waiting in line to view this life-changing masterpiece. In fact, if your home is like mine, you have several choices of Bibles. Let's not let them become museum pieces or dust collectors. Instead, let's daily invest ourselves in the pages that we might become true works of art at the hands of the Creator.

Patsy Clairmont

*S*cripture is one long, beautiful story of God's patient, perfect, lavish love for humankind. And it's not just a fairy tale! Christ bled and died and rose again so we could know, beyond a shadow of a doubt, that God loves us! Sometimes his love doesn't look the way we want it to at the moment; sometimes we have to wait for answers to our prayers. But his grace is ever-present and his love is never-ending.

Barbara Johnson

God's Word will stand forever. It is more than an Old and New Testament compiled into sixty-six books that constitute a divine library. It is a source of guidance, strength, encouragement, and comfort, available every day of our lives. From the ancient sands of Israel to the shores of the New World, the Bible always has been an incredible story of faith and sacrifice. Even when it was banned, burned, and barred from the reading public, God's truth could not be crushed or stopped.

Take a few minutes today to spend with Yahweh. Find the comfort and guidance you need from God's words of direction for that disturbing circumstance in your life. His words are there, and they're written *just for you.*

Luci Swindoll

MEDITATIONS ON GOD'S WORD

Great peace have they who love your law,
*   and nothing can make them stumble.*

I wait for your salvation, O LORD,
*   and I follow your commands.*

PSALM 119:165–166

"As the rain and the snow
*   come down from heaven,*
and do not return to it
*   without watering the earth*
and making it bud and flourish,
*   so that it yields seed for the sower and bread for*
the eater,
so is my word that goes out from my mouth:
*   It will not return to me empty,*
but will accomplish what I desire
*   and achieve the purpose for which I sent it,"*
*   declares the LORD.*

ISAIAH 55:10–11

The Peace of Christ

BESIDE
QUIET WATERS

THE PRINCE OF PEACE

*W*hatever marches into your day, remember who is the Lion of Judah and the Lamb of God. He tallies our days and tends our nights. He who paid the ultimate price to give us life holds us safely in his eternal hands.

Patsy Clairmont

*P*eace. *Isn't that what we all want?*
Peace can be yours right this minute because we have the Peace Maker, Jesus Christ, here with us. He shed his precious blood so you could have peace. If you accept him as your Savior right now, I promise you he will place peace in your heart.

You might be going through a scary situation right now, right in your own heart. But God has not given you a spirit of fear, "but of power, and of love, and of a sound mind" (2 Timothy 1:7 KJV). Repeat this verse over and over again, and then walk boldly in fearless love.

Thelma Wells

We all go through storms in life. Whether we are caught up in the agitation of little daily traumas that tear away at our peace of mind, or face real fears raging within our hearts, Jesus can calm any storm with a word: "Quiet, be still!" (Mark 4:39). When the disciples first witnessed Jesus' power to bring peace, they were amazed: "Who is this? Even the wind and the waves obey him!" (Mark 4:41). We will be amazed, too.

The gift of peace can come quietly, unexpectedly—as you gaze at the soft glow of a candle during a hushed quiet time, as you walk in the woods and feel God close. It can come even in a glimpse out the window, as your eye beholds the beauty outside. It can come through the loving gesture of a friend. It can come through laughter or tears ... or simply silence. It can come through prayer. "Peace be to you," Jesus says. To *you*.

Betsy Lee

Paul wrote, Aim for perfection, listen to my appeal, be of one mind, live in peace. And the God of love and peace will be with you.

2 CORINTHIANS 13:11

MEDITATIONS ON
THE PRINCE OF PEACE

To us a child is born,
*   to us a son is given,*
*   and the government will be on his shoulders.*
And he will be called
*   Wonderful Counselor, Mighty God,*
*   Everlasting Father, Prince of Peace.*

ISAIAH 9:6

Rejoice greatly, O Daughter of Zion!
*   Shout, Daughter of Jerusalem!*
See, your king comes to you,
*   righteous and having salvation,*
*   gentle and riding on a donkey,*
*   on a colt, the foal of a donkey....*
He will proclaim peace to the nations.
*   His rule will extend from sea to sea*
*   and from the River to the ends of the earth.*

ZECHARIAH 9:9–10

Christ himself is our peace.

EPHESIANS 2:14

IMMANUEL, GOD WITH US

*S*torms arise in our lives. A telephone call brings sudden jolting news. A letter brings disappointment. A child has an accident. A small pain develops into a serious illness. Death … divorce … financial reverses. Or maybe the source of distress is just the everyday pressures and tensions that build and build until the thunderhead erupts into a storm.

I, too, have had my share of storms. Some have been brief afternoon showers. Others have been caused by tensions that have built up, threatening my serenity and peace. Still others have burst upon my life suddenly, hitting hard and leaving in their wake damage and debris. Like the disciples, I have been afraid and have cried out, "Lord, don't you care?" And later, when all is calm again, I hear him say, "Gigi, why do you have so little faith?"

He has never promised a life free from storms, but he has promised to be with us in the midst of them and to bring us safely to the other side if we believe in him and rely on him.

Gigi Graham Tchividjian

*D*oes God ever seem too far away, too fearsome, too holy? How can this kind of God be a comfort to you? You know in your mind that God can be trusted, yet your heart resists. Jesus knows your fears and doubts. He came to this earth to show you the Father. He came so you could know him and know the Father's heart—a heart of love, gentleness and compassion. When you know Jesus, you also know the Father.

Jesus loves you passionately, tenaciously, and unconditionally. He doesn't depend on e-mail or the telephone to communicate with you. He is never out of the country when you call. He is closer than the air you breathe. If you are running from God because of your past or present lifestyle, he invites you to let him give you peace and rest. He will never leave you or forsake you, because his perfect love is fearless. There is nowhere he's afraid to go, no part of you he's afraid to face.

Thelma Wells

MEDITATIONS ON IMMANUEL, GOD WITH US

*The rising sun will come to us from heaven ...
to guide our feet into the path of peace.*

LUKE 1:78–79

*The virgin will be with child and will give
birth to a son, and they will call him
Immanuel—which means, "God with us."*

MATTHEW 1:23

*Christ Jesus, being in very nature God,
did not consider equality with God something
to be grasped,
but made himself nothing,
taking the very nature of a servant,
being made in human likeness.*

PHILIPPIANS 2:5–7

*Jesus said, "Surely I am with you always, to
the very end of the age."*

MATTHEW 28:20

GIVING TO THE LORD

*S*he had given her coins in secret, thinking no one saw. Unknown to her, Jesus watched and made note of her gift. "Calling his disciples to him, Jesus said, 'I tell you the truth, this poor widow has put more into the treasury than all the others'" (Mark 12:43).

He alone knew how much it had cost her. *Everything*. She gave not just her money, but also her heart, her trust, her daily bread, her future. He alone knew how much she had gained—the freedom of a child of God leaning wholly on her Creator. Her act was praiseworthy in his sight.

Life is unpredictable. We never know when we might come to the end of our resources—financial, emotional, mental or spiritual. We may think ourselves alone in our struggle, but the Lord is always watching. In our time of need, we can remember this dear widow who so blessed the Lord. She brought everything she had and laid it at his feet. She left with everything she needed, her hand in his.

*Y*ou don't have to be wealthy to start giving to the poor. You don't have to be perfectly organized to start giving of your time. You don't have to have a beautiful home to invite other people in. You don't have to be especially gifted to start making a difference in this world.

If you don't have it all together, join the club. You want to minister or start on the road to success? Use what you have. Begin with the things in your hands. As you give out of your emptiness or loneliness, the gifts flow back your way. It's a mystery, but when Jesus said, "Streams of living water will flow from within" (John 7:38), he was talking about a constant source of energy, love, and enthusiasm. So don't wait another minute to give from what you have; begin today.

Don't wait to start smiling if you're feeling blue. The Lord gives us a face, but it's up to us to provide the expression. And once the joy of giving gets in your system, it's bound to break out on your face.

Barbara Johnson

MEDITATIONS ON GIVING TO THE LORD

Jesus said, "Give, and it will be given to you. A good measure, pressed down, shaken together and running over, will be poured into your lap. For with the measure you use, it will be measured to you."

LUKE 6:38

Whoever sows generously will also reap generously. Each man should give what he has decided in his heart to give, not reluctantly or under compulsion, for God loves a cheerful giver. And God is able to make all grace abound to you, so that in all things at all times, having all that you need, you will abound in every good work.

2 CORINTHIANS 9:6–8

*A gift opens the way for the giver
    and ushers him into the presence of the great.*

PROVERBS 18:16

JESUS, THE GREAT SHEPHERD

*R*ush, rush, rush. Your day is bursting at the seams. There's never enough time to accomplish everything on your to-do list. There's no time to enjoy a sunset, to stand for even five minutes simply feeling the wind on your face. So who has the time to just sit before God with no words, no agenda, no schedule?

Psalm 23 is a wonderful example of true meditation. Jesus, the shepherd, leads you into a beautiful pasture near a quiet stream. It is here, in this tranquil setting, that Jesus refreshes you spiritually. He guides you in his ways and walks with you through even the darkest, most difficult times. You have no need to fear—his authority and power are a comfort to you. He prepares a lavish banquet for you under the shade of the trees. He seats you in a place of honor and sends goodness your way for as long as you live. And with your death will come the joy of living in his presence forever.

Take your wounded, battle-weary heart to Jesus and just sit with him awhile. This can be a time to bask in God's presence and to enjoy who he is and who you are in him.

The parable of the lost sheep, Luke 15:3–7, is often interpreted as follows: Jesus goes out looking for unbelievers, and when they come to salvation, he and the angels rejoice. But think about this parable from a different perspective. The lost sheep is already one of Jesus' sheep. It is not from a different pen and does not belong to a different shepherd. This sheep belongs to Jesus, yet it wanders away and becomes temporarily lost. Jesus' response to lost sheep is always the same: "I myself will search for my sheep and look after them … I will rescue them … and gather them … and I will bring them into their own land" (Ezekiel 34:11–13). Jesus sees wandering sheep as a priority.

Do you know a wandering sheep? Are you one yourself? Jesus will never throw up his hands in frustration and leave you to your own devices. He will come running to find you. "He tends his flock like a shepherd: He gathers the lambs in his arms and carries them close to his heart; he gently leads those that have young" (Isaiah 40:11). This is your Savior, your shepherd, your friend.

MEDITATIONS ON JESUS, THE GREAT SHEPHERD

The LORD is my shepherd, I shall not be in want.
He makes me lie down in green pastures.

PSALM 23:1–2

He will stand and shepherd his flock
in the strength of the LORD,
in the majesty of the name of the LORD
his God.
And they will live securely, for then his greatness
will reach to the ends of the earth.
And he will be their peace.

MICAH 5:4–5

Jesus said, "I am the good shepherd; I know
my sheep and my sheep know me—just as the
Father knows me and I know the Father—
and I lay down my life for the sheep."

JOHN 10:14–15

Our Savior

I have a deep appreciation for the Mackinac Bridge because it led me and kept me connected to Les prior to our marriage. I lived in a suburb of Detroit in the bottom of Michigan's Lower Peninsula, and Les lived in a tiny town at the top of the Upper Peninsula. The Mackinac Bridge united the Upper and Lower Peninsulas, and us.

This famous bridge arches over the spot where Lakes Huron and Michigan merge. If you throw a quarter over one side, your money will be deposited in the Huron while a coin off the other side ends up officially in Lake Michigan. Hmm, the bridge brought together two lakes, two peninsulas, two sweethearts, and two families. No wonder I'm fond of this stretch of metal girders, cables, and highway.

An even greater expanse separates earth and heaven. Christ became our bridge to God. Christ offers us daily assistance, divine opportunities, and eternal provision. He also extends to us his Word, which allows us to arch over this world's distorted mind-set to receive the pure wisdom that is from above.

Speaking of bridges, what about prayer? In quiet conversations with our Lord, we hear in our longing hearts of his expansive love, which helps us to move from our inner conflict to his peaceful resolution.

Patsy Clairmont

When you and I overextended ourselves in sin and owed a debt we could not pay, Jesus paid it in full on the cross of Calvary by shedding his blood, dying, and rising again. Through his blood, we are granted complete pardon and total salvation. We did nothing to deserve it. Because he wanted an intimate relationship with us that could not exist until our debt was paid, our Father sent his only Son to pay off our account. In full.

Marvelous, infinite, matchless grace! It's yours, my friend. Receive it.

Thelma Wells

Jesus came to bring sinners to repentance. He came to save, not to destroy. No matter how hard we try, we will always be sinners until we are with the Lord. First John 1:9 says, "If we confess our sins, he is faithful and just and will forgive us our sins and purify us from all unrighteousness." When you sin, throw yourself on God's mercy. Confess. Humble yourself. He will not excuse you; he will *forgive* you.

MEDITATIONS ON
OUR SAVIOR

There were shepherds living out in the fields nearby, keeping watch over their flocks at night. An angel of the Lord appeared to them, and the glory of the Lord shone around them, and they were terrified. But the angel said to them, "Do not be afraid. I bring you good news of great joy that will be for all the people. Today in the town of David a Savior has been born to you; he is Christ the Lord. This will be a sign to you: You will find a baby wrapped in cloths and lying in a manger."

LUKE 2:8–12

God so loved the world that he gave his one and only Son, that whoever believes in him shall not perish but have eternal life. For God did not send his Son into the world to condemn the world, but to save the world through him.

JOHN 3:16–17

IN THE MIDST OF TURMOIL

*P*eace is something that makes no sense to the uninitiated because it is often peace in the midst of circumstances that cry out: turmoil! I think of the disciples as they huddled together in that small room after Jesus had been executed. They were terrified. They had expected the best and tasted the worst. Peter—loud, salt of the earth, brash, strong, his mouth still sour from his denials that he'd ever met Jesus—was sick to his stomach, sick at heart. And the others were no better: sad, disillusioned, a traveling band with no map, compass, or direction.

And then ... into their silent hell he came walking. Jesus was alive! They still didn't understand anything very well, but Jesus was alive so everything was different. Do you remember what he said to them? "On the evening of that first day of the week, when the disciples were together, with the doors locked for fear of the Jews, Jesus came and stood among them and said, 'Peace be with you!'" (John 20:19). That changed everything for them. They had been falling out of the sky when suddenly Jesus was under them, above them, all around them. That's his promise to us, too.

Sheila Walsh

*D*r. Robert Schuller told of two artists who were commissioned to render a picture depicting peace. One painted a tranquil setting with a mirrored lake that reflected lovely draping trees and a glorious mountain backdrop. Wildflowers filled the surrounding fields while butterflies fluttered about. The scene was picture-perfect.

The other artist painted a thunderous waterfall crashing down onto the jagged rocks below. Next to the waterfall he painted a tree that leaned precariously over the water's edge. One of the tree limbs stretched out close to the threatening falls. There, on the slender twigs of the limb within inches of harm's way, was a nest. In the nest was a mother bird … asleep.

That artist understood that it isn't the absence of problems that demonstrates peace, but being able to rest in the midst of turmoil and threat.

Patsy Clairmont

*A*n optimist is someone who tells you to cheer up when things are going her way. I am more than an optimist. I have been ground in the mill, processed in the plant, and mashed like a potato. I am here to tell you that I am a firm believer in the Bible and its promises. I have learned that grace is not freedom from the storm, but peace within the storm.

Barbara Johnson

MEDITATIONS ON RESTING IN THE MIDST OF TURMOIL

When evening came, Jesus said to his disciples, "Let us go over to the other side." Leaving the crowd behind, they took him along, just as he was, in the boat. There were also other boats with him. A furious squall came up, and the waves broke over the boat, so that it was nearly swamped. Jesus was in the stern, sleeping on a cushion.

MARK 4:35–38

I have set the LORD always before me.
  Because he is at my right hand,
  I will not be shaken.
Therefore my heart is glad and my tongue rejoices;
  my body also will rest secure.

PSALM 16:8–9

ON WINGS OF EAGLES

Our souls were made to "soar on wings" (Isaiah 40:31), and they can never be satisfied with anything short of flying. Like the captive-born eagle that feels within it the instinct of flight, and chafes and frets at its imprisonment, hardly knowing what it longs for, so do our souls chafe and fret, and cry out for freedom. We can never rest on earth, and we long to "fly away" from all that so holds and hampers and imprisons us here.

What, then, are these wings? Their secret is contained in the words, "those who hope in the LORD" (Isaiah 40:31). The soul that hopes in the Lord is the soul that is entirely surrendered to him and that trusts him perfectly. Therefore we might name our wings the wings of Surrender and of Trust. I mean by this, that if we will only surrender ourselves utterly to the Lord and will trust him perfectly, we shall find our souls "soaring on wings like eagles" to the "heavenly places" in Christ Jesus, where earthly annoyances or sorrows have no power to disturb us.

Hannah Whitall Smith

*A*s if Niagara Falls weren't spectacular enough, for more than a century daredevils have been performing all sorts of incredible feats there, trying to win recognition for their courage—if not for their amazing lack of common sense! The most famous of these daredevils was a French tightrope walker known as Blondin, who first crossed the Niagara gorge on a tightrope in 1848.

As believers, we too are tightrope artists, walking Christ's narrow way that stretches straight and true above life's churning waters. We know it's not an easy rope to walk, and we know there are other ways to cross the river. But we choose this one, carefully placing one foot in front of the other and easing out over the abyss.

Occasionally we wobble, but we do not fall. Balanced on the tightrope, high above the chaos, we experience an outrageous peace. And this peace is ours simply because of what we take across the high wire. We take the nail-scarred hand of Jesus and step out confidently over the water, knowing that "the LORD will give strength unto his people; the LORD will bless his people with peace" (Psalm 29:11 kjv).

Barbara Johnson

MEDITATIONS ON SOARING ABOVE IT ALL

Even youths grow tired and weary,
*   and young men stumble and fall;*
but those who hope in the LORD
*   will renew their strength.*
They will soar on wings like eagles;
*   they will run and not grow weary,*
*   they will walk and not be faint.*

ISAIAH 40:30–31

Our light and momentary troubles are
achieving for us an eternal glory that far out-
weighs them all. So we fix our eyes not on
what is seen, but on what is unseen. For what
is seen is temporary, but what is unseen is
eternal.

2 CORINTHIANS 4:17–18

Set your minds on things above, not on
earthly things. For you died, and your life is
now hidden with Christ in God. When Christ,
who is your life, appears, then you also will
appear with him in glory.

COLOSSIANS 3:2–4

THE BREAD OF LIFE

Eve decided: She *would* have that fruit! So Eve accepted the serpent's insinuation that God was holding out on her. We—who still live out the consequences—long to cry, "No! Stop!" And in that pivotal crisis of all time, Adam too chose to eat the forbidden fruit. The serpent inserted a tiny wedge of discontent, which—except for the work of Jesus Christ—opened a chasm of perpetual despair.

The perfect love that had permeated the garden no longer existed in the fallen world; the change was immediate. Adam and Eve scrambled to cover their shame; their oneness with God and with each other shattered. Too late, they discovered that they had traded priceless treasures for empty promises.

Beware of discontent. We all face the temptation to believe there is something better out there. When we accept that belief, we scorn the One who gives us our deepest intimacy and security. Life on earth is flawed. Nothing and no one apart from God can satisfy the aching vacuum in us caused by the fall; only Jesus' love can fill the gap between what is and what was meant to be.

*W*hatever you have in life, if you don't have a relationship with Jesus, you have nothing, absolutely nothing. No relationship or object will touch the ache inside your heart. That ache is the shape of eternity.

Sheila Walsh

*J*esus spoke of spiritual life as abundant life ... a life marked by deep joy regardless of circumstances, of real contentment instead of driving restlessness, an all-is-well relationship with God that leads to profound inner peace, commitment and connection to other people on a soulish intimate level, beauty that transcends age, wealth that is more than material.

We were created for that kind of beauty—the beauty of a life formed to God's heart. If that touches a deep chord of longing in you then I hope you will be increasingly aware that only a well-tended soul produces beauty for life.

Valerie Bell

MEDITATIONS ON
THE BREAD OF LIFE

Jesus declared, "I am the bread of life. He who comes to me will never go hungry, and he who believes in me will never be thirsty."

JOHN 6:35

Jesus said, "I have come that they may have life, and have it to the full."

JOHN 10:10

Jesus said, "I am the living bread that came down from heaven. If anyone eats of this bread, he will live forever."

JOHN 6:51

The Lord Jesus, on the night he was betrayed, took bread, and when he had given thanks, he broke it and said, "This is my body, which is for you; do this in remembrance of me."

1 CORINTHIANS 11:23–24

Jesus Knows How You Feel

*B*etrayal. It is ugly and has devastation as its constant companion. It produces shock, then questioning, anger, numbness and, finally, deep and excruciating pain. Betrayal causes such pain because it is the act of someone trusted and loved. Usually the relationship between the betrayer and the betrayed is forever damaged because betrayal results in the loss of faith and trust.

Have you been betrayed? If so, you need to know that there is, indeed, someone who is faithful, someone you can always count on. Meet Jesus, who is also called "Faithful and True" (Revelation 19:11).

If you have been betrayed, you may feel that no one truly understands your pain. But Jesus does. He is betrayed by one of his closest friends.

If you are in that dark place of betrayal, know that Jesus understands. You can share your pain, confusion and doubts with him. His arms are open wide, waiting to embrace you and ease your pain.

*T*he Lord is not taken aback by our hostilities but instead takes us back ... to Calvary. There he suffered the impact of a cruel and torturous cross. He knows about abuse and pain—and the anger such treatment causes. On the cross, he paid the price for our hostilities and provided the way for our freedom.

Patsy Clairmont

*J*esus, who said, "If you have seen me you have seen the Father," experienced every feeling, every nuance of emotion, every temptation on this earth that you and I do. If this truth is a reality to us, we can't help but be humbled by his graciousness in continually working to conform us to his image. What an awesome privilege that in our rebellious state he loves us and welcomes us always as part of the family—not because of what we do, but because of what he did on the cross.

Marilyn Meberg

MEDITATIONS ON JESUS' EMPATHY

Since we have a great high priest who has gone through the heavens, Jesus the Son of God, let us hold firmly to the faith we profess. For we do not have a high priest who is unable to sympathize with our weaknesses, but we have one who has been tempted in every way, just as we are—yet was without sin.

HEBREWS 4:14–15

Jesus shared in their humanity so that by his death he might destroy him who holds the power of death—that is, the devil—and free those who all their lives were held in slavery by their fear of death.... For this reason he had to be made like his brothers in every way, in order that he might become a merciful and faithful high priest in service to God, and that he might make atonement for the sins of the people. Because he himself suffered when he was tempted, he is able to help those who are being tempted.

HEBREWS 2:14–18

THE LORD LISTENS

*J*esus is waiting for us. He wants to talk to us in our everyday activities—putting on makeup, changing diapers, driving to work or taking a walk. He'll listen to all our questions and opinions and put up with our attitudes. Then—when we stop our chatter for just a moment—he'll reveal our deepest need—and meet it.

Some of us think that the Lord has so many important things to do that our petty problems can wait. The truth is, we don't need an appointment with him. He is always available. Our faith blesses him, and his foremost purpose for us until he returns is to make us his "pure, spotless bride." Don't hold back. Press in. He *wants* to make us clean and whole.

*P*raying does not depend on mental gymnastics or lofty theological abstractions. It is more like banter or inner argumentation or storytelling. As long as it is real, as long as we hide nothing from God of what we are really feeling—anger and joy, frustration and thanksgiving—our prayer is good. God sees the innocent child in us and our rebellious pride. God hears our pleas for forgiveness and our craving for revenge. God accepts our worry words and our surrender, our selfish motives and our selfless moments.

Susan Muto

*P*rayer is effective and loaded with grace. When confronted with an overwhelming circumstance, we say, "All we can do is pray." It is enough. It is more than enough. It unlocks the presence and power of God himself.

Ask and you will receive, and your joy will be complete.

JOHN 16:24

MEDITATIONS ON PRAYER

Jesus said, "I will do whatever you ask in my name, so that the Son may bring glory to the Father. You may ask me for anything in my name, and I will do it."

JOHN 14:13–14

This is the confidence we have in approaching God: that if we ask anything according to his will, he hears us. And if we know that he hears us—whatever we ask—we know that we have what we asked of him.

1 JOHN 5:14–15

Whatever you ask for in prayer, believe that you have received it, and it will be yours.

MARK 11:24

Jesus said, "If two of you on earth agree about anything you ask for, it will be done for you by my Father in heaven. For where two or three come together in my name, there am I with them."

MATTHEW 18:19–20

OUR REDEEMER

*T*he Moabite Ruth was as welcome in Bethlehem as a roach raiding the pantry. Naomi, Ruth's mother-on-law, had tried to dissuade Ruth from following her, convinced that Ruth had a more promising future in Moab.

Ruth was aware of the initial resentment against her in Bethlehem, but she refused to accept rejection. Instead, she placed herself in the Lord's hands as she went out to glean in the fields of any "in whose eyes I find favor" (Ruth 2:2). By "chance" she chose the fields of Boaz, a relative of Naomi's late husband, by Israelite law a kinsman-redeemer and one Israelite with a heart big enough to overlook her Moabite heritage.

When Ruth decided to give her life to the God of Israel, she also decided to trust his people. And God blessed her. He placed her with trustworthy people who had her best interests at heart—and who feared God.

What can we find in Ruth's character to emulate? Everything. We too can refuse to accept the rejection that the world uses to keep us from following hard after God. We have a Kinsman-Redeemer far greater than Boaz. The Lord Jesus Christ will advise, protect and provide for us for the rest of our lives. Count on it.

*A*t one point in my life, I, like a necklace, had frayed until finally my life fell apart. My emotions, like skittish pearls, ricocheted off walls, which left me unstrung. I didn't understand why I was so emotionally frail and fearful or why those around me weren't able to help me gather up my broken parts and put me back together.

But guess what I learned? Jesus is the only true Redeemer. He is the only one who can restring my life and yours, who can retrieve all that we've lost, and who can give us back our value.

Christ assisted me in finding my lost and hidden emotions. Pearl by priceless pearl, he restrung my necklace. He taught me to trade in my panic for the pearl of his peace, to switch my weakness for the pearl of his strength, and to exchange my fear for the pearl of his fearlessness.

I learned I was priceless to him because of his boundless love for me. And that's how he feels about you! So, no matter how unstrung you feel, or how many pearls you've lost, he longs to gather you up in his arms and calm your every fear.

Patsy Clairmont

MEDITATIONS ON OUR REDEEMER

I know that my Redeemer lives,
  and that in the end he will stand upon
the earth.
And after my skin has been destroyed,
  yet in my flesh I will see God;
I myself will see him
  with my own eyes—I, and not another.
  How my heart yearns within me!

JOB 19:25–27

A highway will be there;
  it will be called the Way of Holiness....
Only the redeemed will walk there,
  and the ransomed of the LORD will return.
They will enter Zion with singing;
  everlasting joy will crown their heads.
Gladness and joy will overtake them,
  and sorrow and sighing will flee away.

ISAIAH 35:8–10

"MY PEACE I GIVE YOU"

*I*n Psalm 23 David points out that he had to be led by the Lord to the still waters. I wonder if David had to be led because he was naturally drawn to the excitement of the rushing water?

It certainly is that way with us. Left to our own agendas, we either run at breakneck speed right past the pasture, enamored with our frenzied pace, or sit in parched misery. The Shepherd, who understands our naiveté and our humanity … intervenes on our behalf to guide us with a strong hand onto a quiet path and into a calmer faith.

Perhaps that is why the Lord brought David to the pasture and the water's edge. He knew this young boy would one day be an influential king, and he would need to know how to be still, understanding, attentive, courteous, and calm. The Lord knew David would have to deal with critical issues both politically and personally. He knew the king would need to know where to go when life became too much, when he needed to be restored in his soul, when he just plain needed a break.

Patsy Clairmont

THE *Peace* OF CHRIST

*E*ach of Paul's letters begins with a greeting of peace. Some, like the second one to the Christians in the Greek city of Thessalonica, end the same way. These words were full of meaning. Paul was reminding the Thessalonians that the Lord, the author of peace, would give his peace always, in every way and under all circumstances.

The Thessalonians claimed this peace, and proved it to be applicable and sufficient in their varied situations. This peace lifted them above their problems. In spite of pressure and adversity, their faith grew so that they became examples to others.

Even today we can draw comfort from the experiences of those who have gone before us. We can try to follow their good example, learn not to lose heart, and nurture hope.

Gien Karssen

*T*here is One who ... longs for us to know his rest. He understands our desire for a hiding place. He woos us to his soothing side— even when it's him we've foolishly been hiding from—so that we might find the refuge we so desperately need.

Patsy Clairmont

MEDITATIONS ON
JESUS' PEACE

*Jesus said, "Peace I leave with you; my peace
I give you. I do not give to you as the world
gives. Do not let your hearts be troubled and
do not be afraid."*

JOHN 14:27

*Christ came and preached peace to you who
were far away and peace to those who were
near. For through him we both have access to
the Father by one Spirit.*

EPHESIANS 2:17–18

*Jesus said, "I have told you these things, so
that in me you may have peace."*

JOHN 16:33

*Let the peace of Christ rule in your hearts,
since as members of one body you were called
to peace.*

COLOSSIANS 3:15

THE LORD'S REST

"Busy" is becoming the universal response to "How are you?" in today's fast-paced world. People seem to rate their worth and recognition on the relentless busyness of their schedules. Who has time for a contemplative thought when every moment is filled with activity? And who would ever consider the idea of rest?

The finished work of Jesus Christ on the cross makes it possible for you to enter his rest. There's no need to struggle, no need to fill your life with busywork. You can rest in Christ.

Does the state of the world discourage you? Are you tired of struggling with sin? There is hope. You will live in a kingdom of perfection—for all eternity. But even now you may taste that kingdom during times of spiritual communion with Jesus. When you experience and enjoy God, you taste the glory to come.

Times spent in prayer can be a taste of heaven. Sit quietly for a few minutes. Ask the Holy Spirit to reveal anything that is holding you back from knowing God and the measure of kingdom life that is possible here on earth. Allow Jesus to refresh you and give you strength. Thank him for your taste of heaven and that you will be with him eternally to know him even better.

A yoke is a wooden frame placed across the necks of two animals (often oxen), so they can work together. Often a young, inexperienced ox is trained in a yoke with an experienced, older ox. The stronger ox bears most of the weight and sets the pace. If the younger ox tries to run ahead, fall behind or pull away, it gets a stiff neck, but it is still connected to the older, steady ox. Eventually the younger one will learn from the older one.

Are you looking for rest? Go to Jesus. Jesus wants you to voluntarily take his yoke and learn from him (Matthew 11:29). You may get a stiff neck at times from trying to go your own way, but his gentleness will continually guide you in the right direction. In him you will find rest for your weary soul.

MEDITATIONS ON THE LORD'S REST

Jesus said, "Come to me, all you who are weary and burdened, and I will give you rest. Take my yoke upon you and learn from me, for I am gentle and humble in heart, and you will find rest for your souls. For my yoke is easy and my burden is light."

MATTHEW 11:28–30

The promise of entering his rest still stands ... ... We who have believed enter that rest.

HEBREWS 4:1,3

There remains, then, a Sabbath-rest for the people of God; for anyone who enters God's rest also rests from his own work, just as God did from his. Let us, therefore, make every effort to enter that rest.

HEBREWS 4:9–11

Jesus told his disciples, "Come with me by yourselves to a quiet place and get some rest."

MARK 6:31

JESUS, OUR ALL IN ALL

*I*t's easy to be fooled into thinking our needs can be met in worldly pursuits or in people. But careers invariably come to an end. People consistently fail to meet our expectations. Dreams regularly fade away in the daylight.

If we try to find our identity in, or fix our vision on, these things rather than on Christ, our hearts remain restless, our arms vacant, our thoughts unfocused.

It can be remarkably humbling when we realize (for what may seem like the zillionth time) that only the Lord can satisfy our innermost desires. Nevertheless, we can courageously choose— over and over again: We can open our hearts to the Word of God. We can stretch out our empty arms to embrace our loving Redeemer. We can sit down and surrender our distracting thoughts to receive the quiet stillness of the Holy Spirit's presence.

For the hungry, the empty, and the distracted, the message of Christ is the same. Jesus speaks of pardon and forgiveness, of joy and peace, given freely to all who look to him alone to satisfy their needs.

Debra Evans

*M*any of us don't get the one thing we want most in our personal lives. Some of us dream of a husband's love and don't have it, some desire children and don't have them. One of the greatest challenges in life is to accept the compensations God gives and, through Christ, live in faith and without envy, even when we don't get what we desire most deeply.

When we don't get what we deeply desire, it's easy to look only at what we don't have and ignore the good things we do have. Only Jesus Christ can help us rise above our needs and desires to find joy and purpose in loving others.

*T*he "average" woman today is called upon to balance career, church, and community involvement with the changing needs of her family and friends. Thankfully, on any given day, God promises to meet us where we are and never give us more than we can handle.

Debra Evans

MEDITATIONS ON
JESUS, OUR ALL IN ALL

Jesus said, "I am the Alpha and the Omega, the First and the Last, the Beginning and the End."

REVELATION 22:13

Jesus said, "Everyone who drinks this water will be thirsty again, but whoever drinks the water I give him will never thirst. Indeed, the water I give him will become in him a spring of water welling up to eternal life."

JOHN 4:13–14

Delight yourself in the LORD
and he will give you the desires of your heart.

PSALM 37:4

Godliness with contentment is great gain. For we brought nothing into the world, and we can take nothing out of it. But if we have food and clothing, we will be content with that.

1 TIMOTHY 6:6-8

THE PERFECTER OF
OUR FAITH

*W*hen doubts assail you, examine your heart. Is your doubt simply a mental questioning or testing? If so, don't berate yourself. Seek wisdom and continue to test all things. If your doubt arises from hardness of heart, repent and ask God for greater faith. Jesus is the "perfecter of your faith" (Hebrews 12:2). It is only through your trust in him that your faith will be built up, and that your doubts will finally and fully be put to rest.

"God was *gracious* to Sarah"—God gave her a child without regard to what she did. Her laugh of doubt was turned to laughter of joy.

Even our lack of faith doesn't prevent God from keeping his promises and accomplishing what he plans. God is bigger than the weaknesses of men and of women. First Peter 3:6 says, "You are Sarah's daughters if you do what is right and do not give way to fear." The goal is to trust, and the power to trust is from the Lord.

*I*t took enormous faith for Peter to say,
"Jesus! If it's really you, tell me to come
out there with you. I'd like to walk on water,
too." Peter's faith is strong as long as he focuses
on Jesus. But when he gets out in the wind and
waves, concentrating on Jesus is more difficult.
When Peter takes his eyes off Jesus, disaster
quickly follows.

Does your faith seem strong until trouble
comes? Perhaps you take your eyes off Jesus
and start looking too intently at your situation.

In Numbers 21, the Lord sends poisonous
snakes among the Israelites to punish them for
their sins. Their cure: Look up at the snake on
the pole—a symbol of Christ on the cross. When
the disciples doubt that Jesus has risen from the
dead, Jesus says, "Look at my hands and my
feet. It is I myself!" (Luke 24:39). When you are
in difficult circumstances or when you doubt
God, look to Jesus.

MEDITATIONS ON THE PERFECTER OF OUR FAITH

Let us fix our eyes on Jesus, the author and perfecter of our faith, who for the joy set before him endured the cross, scorning its shame, and sat down at the right hand of the throne of God.

HEBREWS 12:2

Jesus told Peter, "I have prayed for you, Simon, that your faith may not fail. And when you have turned back, strengthen your brothers."

LUKE 22:31

The apostles said to the Lord, "Increase our faith!"

LUKE 17:5

Accept him whose faith is weak ... for God has accepted him.... The Lord is able to make him stand.

ROMANS 14:1–4

THE LORD CARES ABOUT YOU

We don't know how many women traveled with Jesus and the disciples throughout Galilee. These women were disciples in the deepest sense of the word. They followed Jesus, gave him their exclusive loyalty, and used their own resources to help provide for the disciples needs.

Most likely the presence of these women offended many in Israel. Jewish tradition did not allow women to study the law with a rabbi. Obviously, Jesus broke the customs of his culture when he invited women to join him and encouraged them to sit at his feet to learn from him (Luke 10:39, 42).

The Father had said, "It is not good for the man to be alone. I will make a helper suitable for him" (Genesis 2:18). While this principle applies most directly to marriage, it is not necessarily exclusive to it. Men need the gifts, perspective and observations of the women in their lives. Godly women complement godly men—in ministry, in work and in service. Though Jesus never married, he affirmed the worth of women. He not only didn't ignore them—as was common in his day—he included them in his life and ministry, teaching them, listening to them, and affirming their worth as children of God.

*T*hink of it! The One who engineered this incredible universe with such exquisite precision that astronomers can predict exactly where and when Halley's comet will appear— This God is my Lord.

Can we imagine that God, who is concerned with so many stupendous things, can possibly be concerned about us? We do imagine it. We hope he is. That is why we turn to him in desperation and cry out, ... "O Lord!" Where else can we possibly turn when we have come to the end of our resources?

Does God love us? Karl Barth, the great theologian, was once asked if he could condense all the theology he had ever written into one simple sentence. "Yes," he said. "I can. 'Jesus loves me, this I know, for the Bible tells me so.'"

Elisabeth Elliot

"You are precious and honored in my sight,
and ... I love you,"
declares the LORD.

ISAIAH 43:4

MEDITATIONS ON THE LORD CARES ABOUT YOU

Jesus said, "Greater love has no one than this, that he lay down his life for his friends."

JOHN 15:13

Jesus said, "As the Father has loved me, so have I loved you."

JOHN 15:9

I pray that you, being rooted and established in love, may have power, together with all the saints, to grasp how wide and long and high and deep is the love of Christ, and to know this love that surpasses knowledge—that you may be filled to the measure of all the fullness of God.

EPHESIANS 3:17–19

SURRENDERING IT ALL TO CHRIST

"Come to me...." When the circumstances of life are beyond our ability to bear them, when there seems to be no way for things to work out, when rapids hit and the boat threatens to capsize at any moment, when a sudden change in life plans cancels our dreams and reroutes the future, Jesus stands before us, and with His arms opened wide, extends this incredible invitation. Surrendering our burdens at His feet and placing each heavy parcel before the cross, we can choose to close our ears to competing commands and confusing directions, and listen for God's voice alone.

Through surrender—bowing before God's mighty throne, laying each struggle before our Father in heaven, casting out all grief and heartache, giving up to Jesus every source of suffering and sin—we participate, with Christ, in his kingdom's victories. We cannot do it on our own. We are not supposed to even try to do it on our own. Heeding the Lord's command to surrender, we are continually surprised to find that, somehow, in a way that is totally beyond our comprehension, *He triumphs through us.*

Debra Evans

*D*on't waste time holding yourself back from completely surrendering to God. God is love. He made you. He'll keep you. He won't give up on you. He has plans for you that will not harm you, but will give you a bright and glorious future. The next time you sing, "I Surrender All," let it be the truth. He's waiting for you to surrender all to him so he can shower you with abundance!

Thelma Wells

*W*hatever this day brings—a nagging backache, a missed appointment, a phone that never quits ringing—God's strength will be sufficient. But the walk of faith requires ongoing surrender to the Lord's loving care.

The grace of surrender helps us to give up the battle when we still feel like fighting, if that is what God requires. It prompts us to lay down our time and talents before Christ's throne when our preference is to "make things happen." Surrender means giving up, as opposed to giving in. Through surrender, there comes a genuine relinquishing of our rights to Jesus Christ as the Lord of our lives. Through surrender, we find grace in the midst of struggle, peace in the aftermath of pain, strength in a place of powerlessness.

Debra Evans

MEDITATIONS ON SURRENDERING IT ALL TO CHRIST

*Submit yourselves, then, to God .... Come
near to God and he will come near to you....
Humble yourselves before the Lord, and he
will lift you up.*

JAMES 4:7–10

*He has showed you ... what is good.
    And what does the LORD require of you?
To act justly and to love mercy
    and to walk humbly with your God.*

MICAH 6:8

Submit to God and be at peace with him.

JOB 22:21

VICTORY IN JESUS

*L*ife is hard, and most people get through it simply by coping. If people are unhappy in marriage, parenthood, career or friendships, they mostly do the best they can. They cope. But is this the way God wants believers to live?

Paul once referred to life as a race (1Corinthians 9:24–27). The goal is not merely to finish the race, but to *win*, to *conquer*. Paul says in Romans 8:37, "We are more than conquerors through him who loved us." Is your goal in life simply to cope, to get through? Or do you want to be a conqueror, an overcomer? How can you be an overcomer, and what does overcoming require?

When trials, troubles, persecutions, disaster or attacks come, don't give in to fear. God will supply the strength you need to overcome in your adversity.

You are an overcomer because of Jesus Christ. "Who is it that overcomes the world? Only he who believes that Jesus is the Son of God" (1 John 5:5); and, "The one who is in you is greater than the one who is in the world" (1 John 4:4). Praise God!

*M*any women today face situations for which they are not prepared. Whether the situation is a frustrating daily task or a difficult struggle, they face it alone. They are single, widowed or married to a man who is uninvolved, whether by choice or necessity. In the absence of a husband, a woman must find the strength and courage to fend off the world and the enemy at the door without the aid a husband might provide. A Christian woman does not need to panic or feel abandoned. She can do what must be done. The Lord is there, providing wisdom, courage and the strength to win the battle.

*A*s the Holy spirit leads us into a deepening awareness of Jesus' lordship over all of life's experiences—no matter how confusing, difficult, or painful our circumstances may become—our thoughts and feelings find a reliable shelter under the covering of Christ's unfailing love and protective authority.

Debra Evans

With God we will gain the victory.

PSALM 60:12

MEDITATIONS ON KNOWING VICTORY IN JESUS

Everyone born of God overcomes the world. This is the victory that has overcome the world, even our faith. Who is it that overcomes the world? Only he who believes that Jesus is the Son of God.

1 JOHN 5:4–5

Thanks be to God! He gives us the victory through our Lord Jesus Christ.

1 CORINTHIANS 15:57

Jesus said, "In this world you will have trouble. But take heart! I have overcome the world."

JOHN 16:33

Victory rests with the LORD.

PROVERBS 21:31

The fruit of the Spirit

LOVE, JOY, PEACE

A GIFT FROM HEAVEN

*P*eace is a fruit of the Spirit. It has to grow. The amazing thing is that it grows in such an unfriendly climate. You stick a mother in an intensive care unit watching over her child—and the last thing you'd expect is peace. But there it is all over her, mixed in with the tears and the sadness. You take a man's job away from him, the source of a significant portion of his identity, his ability to take care of his family—and peace would seem out of place, even unwelcome. But there it is. I have seen it so many times. The record stands for itself. It is a gift.

Sheila Walsh

Jesus said, "Peace I leave with you; my peace I give you. I do not give to you as the world gives. Do not let your hearts be troubled and do not be afraid."

JOHN 14:27

*F*aith is a powerful force. It *changes* things. It provides a way when there is no way, an answer when there is no answer. It turns "no" into "yes." Faith touches God. It is a gift of the Spirit and a sign to unbelievers. We pray for faith when we have none, and we keep asking until God answers.

A warm letter from a friend. A compliment from my boss. An unexpected refund. A comforting Scripture. These arrive as God's good gifts to me. But they usually get overlooked while I'm focusing on what feels like—at least to me—insurmountable trouble. Always, it's trouble that God hasn't solved yet. Often, I complain about his delayed response. But really, my myopic vision isn't fair to him. If I lift my eyes off the problem, I can spot God's gifts all around me. They may not be the answer I'm searching for at the moment, but they're good and continuous gifts that say, "I still love you, my child." They remind me that God doesn't stop caring for me, even though I live with unfulfilled expectations. Now during the hard times, I remind myself to hunt for God's small surprises while I'm waiting for his big solution. It takes my mind off the problem. It helps me to trust him … It encourages me to know that God still cares.

Judith Couchman

I the LORD will be their God … I will make a covenant of peace with them … I will bless them and the places surrounding my hill. I will send down showers in season; there will be showers of blessing.

EZEKIEL 34:24–26

MEDITATIONS ON
A GIFT FROM HEAVEN

*The fruit of the Spirit is love, joy, peace,
patience, kindness, goodness, faithfulness,
gentleness and self-control.*

GALATIANS 5:22–23

*God did not give us a spirit of timidity, but a
spirit of power, of love and of self-discipline.*

2 TIMOTHY 1:7

*You do not lack any spiritual gift as you
eagerly wait for our Lord Jesus Christ to be
revealed.*

1 CORINTHIANS 1:7

*May our Lord Jesus Christ himself and God
our Father, who loved us and by his grace
gave us eternal encouragement and good
hope, encourage your hearts and strengthen
you in every good deed and word.*

2 THESSALONIANS 2:16–17

WONDERFUL COUNSELOR

Have you ever felt like Job? Wishing for an arbitrator or mediator between you and God? Well, you have one. Jesus understands you, sympathizes with your struggles and has gone to heaven on your behalf so that you can approach God's very throne with confidence (Hebrews 4:14–16). You also have another helper. The Holy Spirit speaks to God on your behalf when you simply don't know how to express your need. God has provided for you. You can go to him—even with your doubt, fear or anger.

It's easy to forget just how exalted and how powerful God is. When you don't understand what God is doing in your life, it's easier to grab the phone and call a friend than to call on God. When you're troubled, go to the One who has all the answers. Go outdoors to pray and praise. Look around; see the power and the glory of God. Remember, these things are but a whisper of him, very faint.

Spiritually, you already are seated with Christ in the heavenly realms. You have been given the Holy Spirit as your helper and teacher. The Spirit will reveal the things of God to you so that you can overcome the obstacles in your life.

*E*verybody should have a friend like Ralph. He can fix a lamp or a lawn mower, refinish furniture, build bookshelves. ...
One day I asked, "Ralph, where did you learn to do all this? Who taught you—your father?"

"I never knew my father," he said. "But I did meet a good carpenter a long time ago. And he still helps me. In fact, every time I have a problem, all I have to do is stop and ask him, 'Teach me what I need to know.' And he does. This morning, for instance, those boards just wouldn't work. But after I'd stopped and asked him, 'What am I doing wrong?' the answer came: I was cutting them too short." Then Ralph gave me the words of his own special prayer:

Jesus stand beside me.
Guide and direct my life.
Teach me what I need to know.
Help me with my work.
Let me serve You and others.
That I may be worthy of God's grace.

Ralph's special prayer has become a part of my own life now. I say it every morning. And all day. Whenever I am anxious or confused about a situation, one phrase of the prayer comes to my rescue: "Teach me what I need to know." Of all the things Ralph has done to help me, his prayer has helped most of all.

Marjorie Holmes

MEDITATIONS ON OUR WONDERFUL COUNSELOR

Jesus said, "I will ask the Father, and he will give you another Counselor to be with you forever—the Spirit of truth. The world cannot accept him, because it neither sees him nor knows him. But you know him, for he lives with you and will be in you."

JOHN 14:16–17

Jesus said, "The Counselor, the Holy Spirit, whom the Father will send in my name, will teach you all things and will remind you of everything I have said to you."

JOHN 14:26

When he, the Spirit of truth, comes, he will guide you into all truth. He will not speak on his own; he will speak only what he hears, and he will tell you what is yet to come.

JOHN 16:13

A GENTLE WHISPER

*I*magine actually hearing the voice of God! Moses seems to accept this as a normal occurrence. And, in fact, it is normal for Moses. The words "the LORD said to Moses" appear 138 times in the Old Testament, the words "the LORD said," 290 times. God wasn't silent then, and he's not silent today. Even though he might not speak audibly, God still has much to say to us.

God is a person. He wants to have a relationship with you. A good relationship requires communication. In other words, he may be speaking, but are you listening? And if you're listening, are you testing the voice to see if it is God's?

During your prayer time, listen for the Lord to speak to your heart, perhaps through a Bible verse, a song, a mental impression or a reaction of some kind. You may sense a response in yourself of faith, awe, peace, praise or healing. The Spirit speaks to the core of your being, filling that deep place in you—that place no one else can reach.

*M*editation can be a wonderful way to enjoy God and to listen to his voice. God has chosen to reveal his thoughts to his people. But often the noise of the world dulls your spiritual ears to the whispers of God. Meditation is an excellent way to still your spirit so that you can be receptive to the Holy Spirit's voice.

Christian meditation is different from all other forms. Christian meditation involves fixing your eyes on Jesus and filling your mind with the things of God; the goal is to commune with God, submitting your will to his.

Find a place where you can be alone. Still your heart and mind by using the scene in Psalm 23. Be very quiet; put aside the noise, busyness and duties of your day, and allow the Spirit of God to refresh your spirit. Take your wounded, battle-weary heart to Jesus and just sit with him awhile. This can be a time to bask in God's presence and to enjoy who he is and who you are in him.

*O*nce we settle down, quiet the noise within and the noise without, and spend time tuning in to God, we come away from that golden communication refined. We've given up our burdens, shored up our faith, lifted up our prayers, stored up Scripture in our hearts, and now we're shined up to reflect God. Our internal experience with God leads to an external expression of him.

Luci Swindoll

MEDITATIONS ON GOD'S GENTLE WHISPER

A great and powerful wind tore the mountains apart and shattered the rocks before the LORD, but the LORD was not in the wind. After the wind there was an earthquake, but the LORD was not in the earthquake. After the earthquake came a fire, but the LORD was not in the fire. And after the fire came a gentle whisper.

1 KINGS 19:11–12

Jesus often withdrew to lonely places and prayed.

LUKE 5:16

*Today, if you hear his voice,
    do not harden your hearts.*

HEBREWS 4:7

"Speak, LORD, for your servant is listening."

1 SAMUEL 3:9

POWER FROM ON HIGH

The power to obey ... isn't that what we all need? It wasn't just the Israelites who blew it repeatedly and had to be jerk-chained back into line; it's every human being who's ever lived. We lack the power to obey.

It is the Holy Spirit of God, living in me, who produces that behavior for which I long, but, paradoxically, sometimes fight against. As Paul says, "I realize that I don't have what it takes. I can will it, but I can't *do* it. I decide to do good, but I don't *really* do it. I decide not to do bad, but then I do it anyway. My decisions, such as they are, don't result in actions" (Romans 7:18–20 MSG). The answer to those struggles lies in accepting the terms of the new covenant: Jesus himself living within me, producing that which I can't.

What is behind that huge relief effort is God's love, a stubborn love that will not let me go, a love so tenacious, so gracious, so unfathomable that he willingly made a new covenant with me at the highest price. That covenant is designed to assure me that in spite of poor performance, I am his and he is mine.

Marilyn Meberg

$\mathcal{W}$e love because God first loved us—and in loving God, we find our greatest delight, our highest joy, our deepest peace, our brightest vision, our strongest shelter. As we live in his love, we welcome the Lord's unchanging, attentive presence and feel at home dwelling in his courts of praise, on good days and bad. Revived and refreshed through prayer and worship, we are renewed with the Spirit's power, no matter what we're going through.

Debra Evans

$\mathcal{T}$he Holy Spirit was present from before the beginning of time, "The Spirit of God was hovering over the waters" (Genesis 1:2). The day of Pentecost is a dividing line in human history, for it is on this day that the Holy Spirit of God becomes available to every Christian man, woman and child. Previously, the Spirit revealed himself only occasionally and for unique works of God. Today, the Spirit never leaves. He lives in us, is ever with us, and gives us the "righteousness, peace and joy" (Romans 14:17) that is such a beautiful evidence of his work in our lives.

MEDITATIONS ON RECEIVING POWER FROM ON HIGH

May the God of hope fill you with all joy and peace as you trust in him, so that you may overflow with hope by the power of the Holy Spirit.

ROMANS 15:13

I pray that out of his glorious riches God may strengthen you with power through his Spirit in your inner being, so that Christ may dwell in your hearts through faith.

EPHESIANS 3:16–17

Jesus said, "You will receive power when the Holy Spirit comes on you; and you will be my witnesses in Jerusalem, and in all Judea and Samaria, and to the ends of the earth."

ACTS 1:8

*N*othing is as sweet as an innocent, trusting baby, and maternal instincts prompt us to protect and cuddle these small ones. Though God is neither male nor female, he expresses the qualities of both genders. This tender description wraps his people in the comfort and security of his eternal love.

Should you encounter bad news today, look within yourself. You'll find God's Spirit, which will enable you to accept graciously that which has been handed to you. Think on those parts of life that are lovely. For even in our saddest days, God is under the sorrow, holding us up.

Help me, Lord, to think on those things
that bring honor to you. Give me joy in my
circumstances so that my life will bring others
joy instead of sadness. Amen

Luci Swindoll

*W*e are not alone along the rugged road … we have the Lord's Spirit to lead us in the way of truth. A lasting source of comfort and joy—the dynamic, indwelling presence of God's supernatural strength. God is with us!

Debra Evans

*S*ometimes when we ask God our Why questions, instead of giving us answers he gives us himself, the Comforter. From Luke 11:13: Even as fathers give good gifts to their children, so our Father gives the best gift, the Holy Spirit, the Comforter, to us as we ask.

Often when we ask God for guidance, what we really want is a guide. My friend told me of a conversation he had with his young son shortly after they moved into their new house. "You can find your way to your new bedroom in the dark by simply turning on the lights in each room as you go." There was an uncertain pause, then, "But, Daddy, won't you please go with me?" Do not be terrified; do not be discouraged, for the LORD your God will be with you wherever you go (Joshua 1:9).

Mary Jane Worden

Shout for joy, O heavens;
rejoice, O earth;
burst into song, O mountains!
For the LORD comforts his people
and will have compassion on his afflicted ones.

ISAIAH 49:13

MEDITATIONS ON
OUR COMFORTER

*The Spirit helps us in our weakness. We do
not know what we ought to pray for, but the
Spirit himself intercedes for us with groans
that words cannot express. And he who
searches our hearts knows the mind of the
Spirit, because the Spirit intercedes for the
saints in accordance with God's will.*

ROMANS 8:26–27

*You, O LORD, have helped me and
comforted me.*

PSALM 86:17

*"I, even I, am he who comforts you,"
declares the LORD.*

ISAIAH 51:12

*Blessed are those who mourn,
for they will be comforted.*

MATTHEW 5:4

LIFE BY THE SPIRIT

Do you want to soar like an eagle? A soaring
eagle doesn't flap its wings frantically in a struggle to stay aloft. It glides on, enjoying the wind,
sweeping effortlessly through the sky. That is
what God has in mind for you. He wants you to
soar on the wind of his Holy Spirit. He wants
you to enjoy the adventure and the scenery.

Don't think you can get up that high? Think
you're too wounded to fly? Listen to what God
did for Jacob (a rotten liar and a deceiver, by the
way): "In a desert land [God] found him, in a
barren and howling waste. He shielded him and
cared for him; he guarded him as the apple of
his eye, like an eagle that stirs up its nest and
hovers over its young, that spreads its wings to
catch them and carries them on its pinions"
(Deuteronomy 32:10–11). That's your God!
Can't fly? Let him carry you. Enjoy the ride—
it's glorious!

*B*umblebees are outrageous because they shouldn't be able to fly, but they do anyway. Their bodies are too heavy and their wingspan is too shallow, but because God is in charge of both bumblebees and aeronautical science, he has enabled bees to defy the laws of aerodynamics. That's what hope is all about: having the confidence that despite your personal limitations and circumstances, God has filled you with his Spirit so you can defy the odds and accomplish his perfect will for your life.

Thelma Wells

*M*any believers find it hard to imagine that they can actually please God. The Scriptures make it quite clear that, indeed, God is thrilled with you at times. According to Colossians 1:10–12, there are four things that please God: bearing fruit in good works, growing in the knowledge of God, having great endurance and patience, and joyfully giving thanks to the Father.

Because God has given you everything you need, by sending the Holy Spirit to dwell in you and by infusing you with his power, you can please him by living a godly life.

MEDITATIONS ON LIVING BY THE SPIRIT

The mind controlled by the Spirit is life and peace.

ROMANS 8:6

Live by the Spirit, and you will not gratify the desires of the sinful nature. For the sinful nature desires what is contrary to the Spirit, and the Spirit what is contrary to the sinful nature. They are in conflict with each other, so that you do not do what you want. But if you are led by the Spirit, you are not under law.

GALATIANS 5:16–18

Those controlled by the sinful nature cannot please God. You, however, are controlled not by the sinful nature but by the Spirit, if the Spirit of God lives in you.

ROMANS 8:8–9

Since we live by the Spirit, let us keep in step with the Spirit.

GALATIANS 5:25

OUR GUARANTEE

*P*aul wrote that God has placed within our hearts a longing for what is not available down here, so that nothing else will do: "Now it is God who has made us for this very purpose and has given us the Spirit as a deposit, guaranteeing what is to come" (2 Corinthians 5:5). If you read this verse in Eugene Peterson's *The Message*, it says, "We've been given a glimpse of the real thing, our true home, our resurrection bodies! The Spirit of God whets our appetite by giving us a taste of what's ahead. He puts a little of heaven in our hearts so that we'll never settle for less."

This seems to be a key to defining our purpose. What we truly long for is just not available this side of heaven. For me this is strangely good news. It's like that annoying missing piece of a puzzle. As I continue to reinterpret the purpose of my life, gaining an understanding of this truth has been life-changing for me. I can stop spending every waking moment searching under the same cushions and through the same drawers for a piece that is not in my possession. I can give myself to something infinitely more worthwhile.

Sheila Walsh

We should be marked, "FRAGILE, HANDLE WITH CARE," yet we are all like packages on a long, hard journey. We have been crushed in the vice grip of personal pain; we have been slammed from every side and become unraveled, unglued, undone, and torn apart at the corners. Instead of being treated like fine china, we have been toe-danced on by a whole herd of elephants!

But there's a wonderful truth that can sustain us as we move forward on this wild ride: we will be claimed by the Master at the end of our trip! Our label may be torn off, our stuffing may be half hanging out, we may even look completely unraveled. But God always recognizes what belongs to him.

So, dear friend, if you are feeling slammed, crushed, broken, undone, unraveled, ripped beyond the point of human endurance … remember that God's mark on you is bold and sure. You may be "damaged goods," but you are *deliverable*. Straight into his open arms. You *will* reach your final destination and be ushered into the presence of the Lord who is eagerly waiting to claim you as his own, once and for all. There is no unclaimed freight in God's kingdom.

Barbara Johnson

MEDITATIONS ON
OUR GUARANTEE

God anointed us, set his seal of ownership on us, and put his Spirit in our hearts as a deposit, guaranteeing what is to come.

2 CORINTHIANS 1:21–22

You also were included in Christ when you heard the word of truth, the gospel of your salvation. Having believed, you were marked in him with a seal, the promised Holy Spirit, who is a deposit guaranteeing our inheritance until the redemption of those who are God's possession—to the praise of his glory.

EPHESIANS 1:13–14

The Spirit himself testifies with our spirit that we are God's children. Now if we are children, then we are heirs—heirs of God and co-heirs with Christ, if indeed we share in his sufferings in order that we may also share in his glory.

ROMANS 8:16–17

GOD'S SPIRIT WITH US

A mother once took her little boy to hear
Paderewski, the great pianist. They had arrived
half an hour early, and eventually the little boy
got restless. Somehow, the mother got absorbed
in reading the program. When she finally looked
up, his seat was empty and he was nowhere to
be seen!

Then ... suddenly she heard the sound of
"Chopsticks." There he was on stage, in the
spotlight, picking away on the long concert
grand!

"Get him out of there!" came voices from
the crowd.

"No!" cried a European accent from the wings,
and the great Paderewski strode on stage. "Boy,
keep going. I'll help you."

And he sat down on the bench next to the little
fellow and began adding fabulous improvisa-
tions—chords, patterns, runs and additional
melodies—as the two of them entranced the
packed house with "Variations on Chopsticks"!

When we pick at our pathetic little prayers—
when we live our pathetic little lives—suddenly
we are not alone. Someone has come alongside
us—none other than the Almighty Spirit of
God!—and we have moved into a duet of greatness beyond our dreams.

Anne Ortlund

I needed assurance from God that he would be with me when I was about to graduate from college, get married six weeks later and then leave with my minister husband to work in Harlem, New York. He gave me that assurance in 2 Corinthians 9:8.

The Lord proved to me over and over that his grace and favor are plentiful. He gave me wisdom and love as I sought to help young people handle the problems of daily living in the midst of poverty. As a result, many found that God is able to help them "abound in every good work."

I found that God was able to quiet fear when I visited one of my students who was very ill in the hospital. She was apprehensive because she was not able to be at home or at school with the rest of her friends. But I prayed with her and said softly when I left, "Mary, don't be afraid, Jesus is in this very room. He is here even though you can't see him." With that assurance of God's ability to care for her, Mary quietly smiled.

Perhaps as you read the "all's" of God in 2 Corinthians 9:8, you might think of some circumstances in your life that seem insurmountable. It's true that sometimes simple, everyday things can loom so large that you feel caught up in a maze with no exit.

In times like these, remember: God is able!

Wanda K. Jones

MEDITATIONS ON GOD'S SPIRIT BEING WITH US

This is how we know that Christ lives in us:
We know it by the Spirit he gave us.

1 JOHN 3:24

God has said,

"Never will I leave you;
never will I forsake you."

So we say with confidence,

"The Lord is my helper; I will not be afraid."

HEBREWS 13:5–6

Jesus said, "I will not leave you as orphans; I
will come to you. Before long, the world will
not see me anymore, but you will see me.
Because I live, you also will live. On that day
you will realize that I am in my Father, and
you are in me, and I am in you."

JOHN 14:18–20

The LORD said, "I will give them an
undivided heart and put a new spirit in them.

EZEKIEL 11:19

CALLED TO BE HOLY

When I was little, my Uncle Jimmy walked me through his watermelon patch in Idabel, Oklahoma. Holding a tiny black seed he said, "These big melons grew from seeds just like this one." That seemed impossible to me! Yet eighty miles from Idabel is Hope, Arkansas, the town where something more "impossible" became reality.

Young Jason Bright gave his watermelon seed proper care and the right environment to grow. The result? A world-record 260-pound watermelon! Watermelon seeds simply do what comes naturally to them—they grow. Their seeds are set apart by God for that purpose.

When you are set apart by God, holiness becomes natural. The Father is the gardener, Christ is the seed. With Christ in you, you will grow to be like him. It is natural for the Lord not to sin. Therefore, with God's seed in you, it becomes increasingly natural for you not to sin. What seems impossible becomes possible. You will not become instantly sinless, but you will sin less and less and less. God calls you to be holy. With his presence inside you, he will produce the impossible through you. Why settle for anything less?

June Hunt

*A*s New Testament people, we no longer build a temple for the Lord. Christ dwells not in a temple of stone, but in the lives of his people—lives dedicated for his use. And we are to build a life that he "may take pleasure in it and be honored" (Haggai 1:8).

It takes careful thought to build a life foundation on God's Word. It takes careful thought to frame a life with prayer. It takes constant prioritizing to "seek first his kingdom" (Matthew 6:33) when so many temptations and decisions confront us. But the rewards are worth all the work. Because when we provide the "perspiration" to build carefully, Jesus Christ provides the "inspiration." He comes to dwell with us. He "decorates" our lives with joy. His Spirit paints our rooms with the colors of peace, patience, goodness, gentleness and self-control.

Ruth DeJagger

*J*esus is coming. We don't know if it is a thousand years away or tomorrow, but Jesus is coming. A new heaven and earth will replace the old. Our confidence that Jesus will return is not meant to draw us into complex speculations on when and where and how. Rather, it should move us into godly living that will honor him.

MEDITATIONS ON OUR CALL TO BE HOLY

May God himself, the God of peace, sanctify you through and through. May your whole spirit, soul and body be kept blameless at the coming of our Lord Jesus Christ. The one who calls you is faithful and he will do it.

1 THESSALONIANS 5:23–24

Do you not know that your body is a temple of the Holy Spirit, who is in you, whom you have received from God? You are not your own; you were bought at a price.

1 CORINTHIANS 6:19–20

Just as he who called you is holy, so be holy in all you do; for it is written: "Be holy, because I am holy."

1 PETER 1:15–16

God who began a good work in you will carry it on to completion until the day of Christ Jesus.

PHILIPPIANS 1:6

SPIRITUAL TRANSFORMATION

While every woman's life story is unique, there are longings of the heart that seem to be universal: the desire to find true love, the desire that someone will affirm our inherent value regardless of our situation, the hope that we can change. In this regard, we each need a Cinderella story of our own. God finds each of us in the cinders of a less than perfect world, held back from the life we dream of living. He longs to raise us up to a high position, transform us and grant us his power, so he seeks us out, inviting each of us to dance with him.

Dancing in the arms of God is a relationship between you and God that is based on love and mutual respect. The two of you communicate in a close, intimate setting. He holds you, but his embrace is the embrace of a lover, not the restraint of an oppressor. As partners in this dance, God leads, and you let him, moving with the flow of his leading. You are not enveloped in God, losing your identity as a unique person; you are who you are, retaining your freedom and individuality at every turn.

Connie Neal

157

When our children were born, my husband and I lovingly cared for them daily. We held them close, rocked them to sleep and fed them. As they were able, we encouraged them to learn to walk, dress themselves and communicate. We watched excitedly as they grew.

Likewise, our heavenly Father is actively involved in our growth; he encourages us according to our capabilities and understanding at the time. He does not push us; he waits until we are ready. If God told us everything about ourselves and life all at once, we would be confused and crushed. Instead he teaches us based on our spiritual and emotional age level. God's gentle unfolding plan increases our insight and encourages our consistent growth.

Lord, you are a compassionate and caring Father. Thank you for nurturing my development step by step and giving me understanding just as I need it. Help me to be as patient as you are with my simple and imperfect attempts at gaining maturity.

Joan C. Webb

MEDITATIONS ON SPIRITUAL TRANSFORMATION

It was God who gave some to be apostles, some to be prophets, some to be evangelists, and some to be pastors and teachers, to prepare God's people for works of service, so that the body of Christ may be built up until we all reach unity in the faith and in the knowledge of the Son of God and become mature, attaining to the whole measure of the fullness of Christ.

EPHESIANS 4:11–13

O LORD, you are our Father.
We are the clay, you are the potter;
we are all the work of your hand.

ISAIAH 64:8

Consider it pure joy ... whenever you face trials of many kinds, because you know that the testing of your faith develops perseverance. Perseverance must finish its work so that you may be mature and complete, not lacking anything.

JAMES 1:2–4

The Gospel of Peace

GOOD NEWS!

BECOMING CHILDREN
OF GOD

*G*od wants to adopt you. Ephesians 1:5 says, "He predestined us to be adopted as his children through Jesus Christ." When did he come up with that plan? "He chose us in him before the creation of the world" (Ephesians 1:4). In other words, before the world was even in place, God determined to be your adoptive Father, and to make that adoption possible through Jesus Christ and his death on the cross.

You can't be adopted without Jesus because you fall short of God's standard for perfection; your born-into-sin state separates you from your heavenly Father. But because Jesus died for your imperfection—not just some of it, but all of it— you can become pure, cleansed, and forgiven of that sin when you confess it and then acknowledge Jesus' death as your payment for that sin. First John 1:9 says, "If we confess our sins, he is faithful and just and will forgive us our sins and purify us from all unrighteousness."

Now that's fantastic, but here's where you have to make a decision. This is where the adoption concept figures in. John 1:12–13 says, "To all who received him, to those who believed in his name, he gave the right to become Children of God."

hildren born not of natural descent, nor of human decision or a husband's will, but born of God." Who's all this for? Those who believe and receive Jesus as Savior. Those people then become the adopted "children of God." It's as if Jesus takes our "ticket" of repentance at the gates of heaven, cleans us up, and then takes us to the Father and says, "Here she is, Father, your totally cleansed, completely forgiven, newly adopted daughter." God stretches out his Father arms, scoops us up into his divine embrace, and says, "Welcome home!"

That is our outrageous position with the Father who loves us unconditionally and never turns away. What makes that truth even more tender is the use of the word *Abba*, which in the Hebrew means "daddy." We never get too old or too sophisticated to at times long for a daddy, one into whose lap we can crawl and be held, soothed, and comforted. Hosea 14:3 says, "In you the fatherless find compassion." We don't find reprimand, rebuke, or criticism in that Daddy lap; we find compassion for our weakness, compassion for our fatigue, compassion for our many questions, and inexhaustible compassion and forgiveness for our sins.

Marilyn Meberg

MEDITATIONS ON BECOMING CHILDREN OF GOD

Everyone who believes that Jesus is the Christ is born of God.

1 JOHN 5:1

God sent the Spirit of his Son into our hearts, the Spirit who calls out, "Abba, Father."

GALATIANS 4:6

Jesus called the children to him and said, "Let the little children come to me, and do not hinder them, for the kingdom of God belongs to such as these."

LUKE 18:16

I thank God every time I remember you. In all my prayers for all of you, I always pray with joy that God who began a good work in you will carry it on to completion until the day of Christ Jesus.

PHILIPPIANS 1: 3–4, 6

PEACE WITH GOD

*T*hunder and lightning, a thick cloud, smoke, loud trumpeting and then the voice of God. The Israelites experience all this when God descends to the top of Mount Sinai. They tremble "with fear" (Exodus 20:18).

Have you experienced the immensity of God's power, majesty and holiness? Few people have—and few want to. It's much more pleasant to think about the beautiful, peaceful, loving face of God than his mightiness, holiness and power. Does God want us to be afraid of him?

To fear God is to acknowledge his holiness and power, to respect and honor him and to stand in awe of him. Those who rebel against God should be afraid of him. Their rebellion incurs his anger. But if you are his child, God does not want you to be afraid of him.

As you draw near to God, he will draw near to you. The time you spend with him is time like no other because he is like no other. If you are afraid, ask God to show himself to you as your loving and compassionate friend. The Holy Spirit will be your helper as you yield to God. Learn to trust him and begin to enjoy his presence.

MEDITATIONS ON HAVING PEACE WITH GOD

"Come now, let us reason together,"
*   says the LORD.*
"Though your sins are like scarlet,
*   they shall be as white as snow;*
though they are red as crimson,
*   they shall be like wool."*

ISAIAH 1:18

Who is a God like you,
*   who pardons sin and forgives the trans-*
gression
*   of the remnant of his inheritance?*
You do not stay angry forever
*   but delight to show mercy.*
You will again have compassion on us;
*   you will tread our sins underfoot*
*   and hurl all our iniquities into the depths*
of the sea.

MICAH 7:18–19

PEACE IN OUR
RELATIONSHIPS

George and I have been married for nearly forty years now, and life gets sweeter every year. My husband is a man among men. My relationship with him is one where love, understanding, happiness, peace, comfort, pleasure, and intimacy is lavished upon me—no strings attached.

But George is not a saint—and neither am I. Like every other couple, we've had some rough times and we've walked on some shaky ground. People sometimes ask me what our "secret" is to staying happily married for so long. Well, there is no question in my mind that the most crucial ingredient to a successful relationship is God's grace. Grace is the glue that keeps George and me together; and it is pure gift. But God also taught us long ago to be gracious to one another. By practicing the art of extending grace at home, we have avoided many of the heartaches we've watched other couples suffer.

It's been over twenty years since George and I have had a fight. Now, I didn't say we've never been angry with each other in those twenty years; I said we haven't fought. You see, you can disagree but remain agreeable. Ruth Bell Graham's wise words apply in every marriage: "It's my job to love Billy. It's God's job to make him good."

Thelma Wells

*A*ccepting others as they are is a perfect picture of seeing theory lived out in practicality. We may say we accept others, but until we actually do it, it is only theory. No one can actually change anyone else, so why do we try so hard? Present to them the gospel? Yes! Attempt to introduce them to Christ? Fine. Suggest a better way of life or standard of living? They'll probably appreciate it. But change them? No.

If we want our associates to change, two things must occur: We must leave their alteration to the work of God—to his Spirit and timing; and we must accept them (preferably love them) as they are.

Luci Swindoll

*S*omething about injustice convinces us of our right to hold onto our anger and even embrace it. I'm learning anger is not necessarily a wrong response ... until I choose to harbor and nurture it. When I enfold anger, it drains my energy and takes up valuable inner space. Brewing anger taxes my physical, mental and emotional well-being. It also hampers my close relationships with others and God.

Patsy Clairmont

MEDITATIONS ON HAVING PEACE IN OUR RELATIONSHIPS

As God's chosen people, holy and dearly loved, clothe yourselves with compassion, kindness, humility, gentleness and patience. Bear with each other and forgive whatever grievances you may have against one another. Forgive as the Lord forgave you. And over all these virtues put on love, which binds them all together in perfect unity.

COLOSSIANS 3:12–14

If it is possible, as far as it depends on you, live at peace with everyone.

ROMANS 12:18

Let your conversation be always full of grace.

COLOSSIANS 4:6

Do not let the sun go down while you are still angry.

EPHESIANS 4:26

EXPERIENCING GOD'S FORGIVENESS

*W*hen God sent his son, Jesus, to live among us and die for our sins, he knew we did not and never would deserve this kind of sacrificial love. He also knew we would continue to mess up until the end of time. We could never save ourselves, so he poured out his life for us and brought us back into the Garden of his love.

What a gift! Knowing that God's Son died a cruel death on an old rugged cross so that I can have an intimate relationship with the Almighty makes me want to reach out my short, chubby arms, grab Jesus around his neck, and hug him the way my grandchildren hug me tight and say, "Grammy, I love you!" Even when they've misbehaved, they can come to me and steal my heart with their sweet embrace.

When we embrace the grace of God, we can come to him with the spirit of a little child and say, "Father, I've messed up. Please forgive me. I love you!" Instantly, faster than a grandmother's pardon, God grants us his unmerited favor through Christ Jesus and loves us freely once more. What a gift!

Thelma Wells

God is calling to you. Are you running to meet him—or are you hiding from him? Shame can prevent an intimate, personal relationship with God. But it's important to differentiate between *true* shame and *false* shame. You feel true shame if you feel guilty for your sin (and all of us sin). You feel false shame if you feel dirty because another person sinned against you. If you have been wounded by someone else's sin, you may feel a sense of shame, but it is not true shame. Bring true shame to the cross of Jesus for forgiveness. Bring false shame into the arms of Jesus for healing .

If your sin seems too great or horrible to be forgiven or if your shame seems so overwhelming that it can't be removed, remember, Jesus loves you so much that he has already taken your sin and shame on himself. He makes you clean from it. Receive his gift and let him wash your shame away.

In spite of your past—no matter what you have done—God loves you and has plans for you (Jeremiah 29:11-14). You can believe him when he says, "I have loved you with an everlasting love; I have drawn you with loving-kindness (Jeremiah 31:3).

MEDITATIONS ON EXPERIENCING GOD'S FORGIVENESS

Blessed is he
*   whose transgressions are forgiven,*
*   whose sins are covered.*
Blessed is the man
*   whose sin the LORD does not count*
against him
*   and in whose spirit is no deceit.*

When I kept silent,
*   my bones wasted away*
*   through my groaning all day long.*
For day and night
*   your hand was heavy upon me;*
my strength was sapped
*   as in the heat of summer.*

Then I acknowledged my sin to you
*   and did not cover up my iniquity.*
I said, "I will confess
*   my transgressions to the LORD"—*
and you forgave
*   the guilt of my sin.*

PSALM 32:1–5

A RELATIONSHIP RESTORED

When Adam and Eve disobeyed their Creator, the whole human race was lost in sin. Then God came down to earth in human flesh as Jesus and claimed us back to himself. Jesus Christ died on a cruel, rugged cross to purchase our salvation through his blood. Those who have accepted him as Lord and Savior have been reclaimed as children of the Most High God! We have been saved from the ravages of sin. We are promised eternal life with God, the Creator; Jesus, his Son; and the Holy Spirit, our ever-present Comforter. Now that's a reason to praise him!

Not only have we been redeemed and saved by the blood of Jesus, but God also delivers us from everyday problems. He rescues us from situations that seem impossible. He often heals our sicknesses and diseases. He calms our anxious hearts. When we have problems, disappointments, and tough decisions to make, he reminds us through his Word that he is in control of it all. No sickness or disease, financial dilemma, loss of a loved one, addiction, distress, peril, disaster, danger, or anything else can ever separate us from his protection, guidance, and boundless love. Now that makes me shout, "Hallelujah!"

Thelma Wells

The ark, the symbol of God's presence, is a curtain separating the Holy Place from the Most Holy Place. The Most Holy Place is where God meets with Moses. The courtyard is for worshippers. Only priests can enter the Holy Place and only the high priest can enter the Most Holy Place.

At Christ's death, the temple curtain was wondrously torn in two from top to bottom. All believers today have access to the Most Holy Place because of the shed blood of Jesus. Christ's blood covers sin and allows believers full access to and intimacy with Almighty God.

Picture Jesus standing between the Holy Place and the Most Holy Place with his arms outstretched, his hands holding the edges of the torn curtain. If you desire to go beyond the curtain, you must walk into his arms. When you do, his arms will enfold you, drawing the edges of the curtain around you, closing you off from everything but his presence. Nothing else will matter. You will be complete in him, enjoying his presence and love.

MEDITATIONS ON A RELATIONSHIP RESTORED

God has reconciled you by Christ's physical body through death to present you holy in his sight, without blemish and free from accusation.

COLOSSIANS 1:22

Create in me a pure heart, O God,
*   and renew a steadfast spirit within me.*
Do not cast me from your presence
*   or take your Holy Spirit from me.*
Restore to me the joy of your salvation
*   and grant me a willing spirit, to sustain me.*

PSALM 51:10–12

If, when we were God's enemies, we were reconciled to him through the death of his Son, how much more, having been reconciled, shall we be saved through his life! Not only is this so, but we also rejoice in God through our Lord Jesus Christ, through whom we have now received reconciliation.

ROMANS 5:10–11

A NEW COVENANT

*S*ince no human being is inherently righteous, no one can enter into fellowship with
God on his or her own. A person's most basic
spiritual need is to be reconciled to God, to be
made right and whole before God. The sole
answer to our dilemma is found in Christ, who
justifies us (makes us right) in God's sight
through our faith in him.

*J*ustification is the sovereign act of God
whereby he declares the believing sinner
righteous. In other words, when a person comes
to God just as she is, God looks at her, and
because of what Jesus Christ did on the cross he
proclaims her righteous. She does not have to
clean up her act. She does not have to do
penance. She does not have to be thin or good-
looking or rich or famous or accomplished.
All she has to do is believe God for the forgiveness of her sins. Salvation is a gift. He gives.
You receive.

Luci Swindoll

*G*od knew his standard was humanly impossible, so he made sure we all knew that, and then made a new covenant—one that provided for us a perfect person (Jesus) who, through his death on the cross, paid the price for our imperfection (sin). When I enter into that covenant relationship with Christ, I am washed with grace and welcomed as one of his people. My imperfection is forgiven and God forgets it.

If I truly believe in the terms of the new covenant, I will recognize that it is the Holy Spirit of God, living in me, who produces that behavior for which I long, but, paradoxically, sometimes fight against. The answer to those struggles lies in accepting the terms of the new covenant: Jesus himself living within me, producing that which I can't. What is behind that huge relief effort is God's love, a stubborn love that will not let me go, a love so tenacious, so gracious, so unfathomable that he willingly made a new covenant with me at the highest price.

Marilyn Meberg

After the supper Jesus took the cup, saying, "This cup is the new covenant in my blood, which is poured out for you."

LUKE 22:20

MEDITATIONS ON THE NEW COVENANT

"The time is coming," declares the LORD,
　　"when I will make a new covenant …
I will put my law in their minds
　　and write it on their hearts.
I will be their God,
　　and they will be my people …
I will forgive their wickedness
　　and will remember their sins no more."

JEREMIAH 31:31–34

Jesus said,

"The Spirit of the Lord is on me,
　　because he has anointed me
　　to preach good news to the poor.
He has sent me to proclaim freedom for the prisoners
　　and recovery of sight for the blind,
to release the oppressed,
　　to proclaim the year of the Lord's favor."

LUKE 4:18–19

TURNING BACK TO GOD

*D*avid committed adultery with Bathsheba and then had Bathsheba's husband, Uriah, killed to cover up what he had done. Nathan the prophet confronts David with his sin. David responds with true repentance and is immediately forgiven (2 Samuel 12:1–14).

True repentance is more than a simple "You're right; I'm sorry." True repentance is a heartfelt recognition of guilt, accompanied by a desire for restoration and a turning away from sin. God forgives David's sin and David devotes himself to the Lord all the rest of his life. He is remembered as one who "had done what was right in the eyes of the LORD and had not failed to keep any of the LORD'S commands all the days of his life—except in the case of Uriah the Hittite".

Are you alienated from God because of sin and disobedience? Return to him. He will not turn away from a broken and contrite heart. Your broken relationship can be restored only if your heart is broken in repentance. Bring the pieces of your heart and your life to Jesus, the only One who can mend them.

*A*fter thirty minutes of calling our cat's name, I heard a faint meow. I kept calling her and walking toward the sound until I found her, hiding behind a bush. I picked her up and carried her home.

We all have wandering hearts. We all hide in closets or under beds and occasionally get outside a safe place … and time after time, God comes looking for us. There is nowhere that you can hide that the boundless love of God can't find you. No matter what kind of mess you get into, he'll be there.

Lily's paws were muddy and my pajamas were covered in dirt. How much more does God allow himself to be covered in our mud, our sin, our messes? But you'll never hear a word of complaint. Just a "Welcome home, you little monkey!" Perhaps you feel as if you have gone too far. Let me assure you, you cannot go too far from God.

So when you hear that quiet call in your spirit in the darkest night of your life when you are lost beyond belief, just let out a little meow. God will find you and carry you home and wash you off and feed you. He will always celebrate your return.

Sheila Walsh

MEDITATIONS ON
TURNING BACK TO GOD

*"Return to me, and I will return to you," says
the Lord Almighty.*

MALACHI 3:7

*"If my people, who are called by my name, will
humble themselves and pray and seek my face
and turn from their wicked ways, then will I
hear from heaven and will forgive their sin and
will heal their land," declares the LORD.*

2 CHRONICLES 7:14

*Rend your heart
    and not your garments.
Return to the LORD your God,
    for he is gracious and compassionate,
slow to anger and abounding in love.*

JOEL 2:13

*While [the prodigal son] was still a long way
off, his father saw him and was filled with
compassion for him; he ran to his son, threw
his arms around him and kissed him.*

LUKE 15:20

GOD LOVES YOU!

God makes all things beautiful for us. He prepares a table before us, even in the presence of our enemies. He provides the Bread of Life to fill our hungry souls. He illuminates the dark places, and he offers us rest. He promises to withhold no good thing from us, and he gives us people to love. He loves us extravagantly, far beyond anything we can comprehend.

Thelma Wells

God's love simplifies all our relational dilemmas. The answer to the people who perplex us is love. God's love, expressed in us, makes us generous of heart. God's love in us transforms our character, enabling us to love a world of lovely and unlovely others. God's love, in us, makes us consistent in character, as kind to the unlovely as to those to whom we are naturally attracted. When we love this way, our souls develop beautifully, connected deeply to both God and to other people. Love is the soul's greatest beautifier!

Valerie Bell

*T*he apostle Paul summed up the bottom-line truth of our lives so beautifully when he recorded with utter confidence one of the most beautiful passages in all of Scripture.

Who shall separate us from the love of Christ? Shall trouble or hardship or persecution or famine or nakedness or danger or sword? ... No, in all theses things we are more than conquerors through him who loved us. For I am convinced that neither death nor life, neither angels nor demons, neither the present nor the future, nor any powers, neither height nor depth, nor anything else in all creation, will be able to separate us from the love of God that is in Christ Jesus our Lord.

ROMANS 8:35, 37–39

Dear one, I urge you to read this love letter of faith and encouragement—the whole of Romans 8—over and over again ... and again ... until you become "convinced," with Paul, that *nothing* can stop the flow of God's tenacious, boundless, outlandish, wildly extravagant love into your life. So much in life is unpredictable, but God's love is certain.

Barbara Johnson

MEDITATIONS ON HOW MUCH GOD LOVES YOU

The LORD shielded him and cared for him;
  he guarded him as the apple of his eye,
like an eagle that stirs up its nest
  and hovers over its young,
that spreads its wings to catch them
  and carries them on its pinions.

DEUTERONOMY 32:10–11

God is love. This is how God showed his love among us: He sent his one and only Son into the world that we might live through him. This is love: not that we loved God, but that he loved us and sent his Son as an atoning sacrifice for our sins.

1 JOHN 4:8–10

God demonstrates his own love for us in this: While we were still sinners, Christ died for us.

ROMANS 5:8

We love because God first loved us.

1 JOHN 4:19

WORDS OF PEACE

*O*n the day of my five-year, cancer-free celebration, a package arrived. I tore open the gift wrapping and discovered the well-worn book, *The Healing Power of Christ*. This profound book—this special message from God—that had been my spiritual food in the most difficult year of my life was in my hands again. I stretched out on my chaise lounge and hoped that no one would interrupt as I opened the pages.

As I'd done five years earlier, I read in no particular order, just grabbing a sentence here and a paragraph there, this time driven by excitement. Nothing jumped from the pages. Nothing at all. Then I started at the beginning, thinking I would read straight through page by page. I found insights and observations worth contemplating, but not at all what I'd remembered.

This book didn't seem worth the reading, much less the effort we had put into finding it. Other than a few choice nuggets, it seemed boring, provincial, and not too well written. I picked it up a few times over the next week or so, read a few pages, and put it down again, shaking my head in wonder at what could possibly have made me think it held life's answers.

*f*inally it came to me, like the lightbulb-over-the-head in the comics, and I ran to get the book.

Page 6: "My grace is sufficient for thee, for my strength is made perfect in weakness (2 Corinthians 12:9 KJV)."

Page 7: "I pray thee, let a double portion of thy spirit be upon me (2 Kings 2:9 KJV)." Oh, how I'd prayed for a double portion. Again on page 7: "... they shall possess the double: everlasting joy shall be unto them (Isaiah 61:7 KJV)." I turned the pages. "Lo, I am with you always, even unto the end of the world (Matthew 28:20 KJV)."

On and on, I uncovered truths that were there, not only before Emily Gardiner Neal wrote *The Healing Power of Christ*, but before the very foundation of the earth.

The secret was found at last! The mystery was a mystery no longer. The comfort and peace— the words that had empowered me to face the most overwhelming interference of my life— came from God's Word, faithfully transcribed by the author because of its application to her own life. My empowerment came from the same Scriptures that I'd been cajoled, bribed, and sometimes badgered to learn as a child in a little fundamentalist church in West Virginia.

Sue Buchanan

MEDITATIONS ON
WORDS OF PEACE

Oh, how I love your law, O LORD!
I meditate on it all day long.
Your commands make me wiser than my enemies,
for they are ever with me.
I have more insight than all my teachers,
for I meditate on your statutes.
I have more understanding than the elders,
for I obey your precepts.
I have kept my feet from every evil path
so that I might obey your word.
I have not departed from your laws,
for you yourself have taught me.
How sweet are your words to my taste,
sweeter than honey to my mouth!
I gain understanding from your precepts.

PSALM 119:97–104

I rise before dawn and cry for help;
I have put my hope in your word, O LORD.
My eyes stay open through the watches of the
night,
that I may meditate on your promises.

PSALM 119:147–48

FREEDOM FROM THE PAST

*M*atthew 1:5 lists Rahab among the fore-
bears of Jesus. But she is not called
"the prostitute," for the stigma of her past is
overshadowed by the honor given her by God.
And by choosing her—a Gentile sinner—God
confirms that he is the Savior of all peoples, for
all time and in all circumstances.

Is there hope for a woman with a past, someone
who has made bad decisions and given herself
to a life of sin? Our enemy wants us to believe
that nothing good can come from such wreckage.
But Rahab's life demonstrates the benefits of
believing *God* instead. When Rahab chose him,
he gave her a completely new life. And he set no
limits on her potential as his child. None.

*O*ur Good Shepherd diligently searches for
those who stray from His tender care,
regardless of how desolate or dangerous their
terrain becomes. No matter what we have done
or how unclean we may feel inside, Jesus is
waiting for us to walk with Him. He will not
condone what we have done, but He will not
condemn us. Instead, He calls us to leave our
old life behind and walk with Him into the light
of eternity.

Debra Evans

*E*ver wish you could start over? Probably all of us have longed for another chance in some area of our lives. We wouldn't necessarily have done things differently, just more or perhaps less ... The truth is we can't go back, only forward into uncharted territory. To sit in our sorrow would lead to misery. Although regret that leads to change is a dear friend, regret that leads to shame is a treacherous enemy.

How do we live without allowing regret to rob us of our joy? How about this insight to prompt us on: "And lean not on your own understanding" (Proverbs 3:5). There is no guarantee that if we had done a part of our lives differently things would end up any different. We have to trust the God of the universe who directs the outcome of all things that he will do that which ultimately needs to be done (in spite of us if necessary).

Patsy Clairmont

MEDITATIONS ON FREEDOM FROM THE PAST

"Forget the former things;
do not dwell on the past.
See, I am doing a new thing!
Now it springs up; do you not perceive it?
I am making a way in the desert
and streams in the wasteland,"
declares the LORD.

ISAIAH 43:18–19

If anyone is in Christ, he is a new creation;
the old has gone, the new has come!

2 CORINTHIANS 5:17

The apostle Paul wrote, "Not that I ... have
already been made perfect, but I press on to
take hold of that for which Christ Jesus took
hold of me.... I do not consider myself yet to
have taken hold of it. But one thing I do:
Forgetting what is behind and straining
toward what is ahead, I press on toward the
goal to win the prize for which God has
called me heavenward in Christ Jesus."

PHILIPPIANS 3:12–14

FINDING HOPE

Many of us have ideas about hope that are simply all wrong—totally contrary to what biblical hope is all about. Either we experience hope as mere wishful thinking, or we cynically dismiss it as child's play.

Hope for the Christian is much more than pie-in-the-sky wishful thinking. The dictionary defines hope as a verb of expectation—to "hope against hope," to actively and confidently expect fulfillment. Hope as a noun is defined as a confident expectation that a desire will be fulfilled. Hope as a virtue is described as the confidence with which a Christian looks for God's grace in this world and glory in the next.

Did you get the common denominator? Hope is all about placing our confidence in what we can't yet see, about having high expectations that, in spite of all appearances to the contrary, our deepest longings will be fulfilled. And as Christians, that's exactly what we can count on.

Thelma Wells

*H*ope uncovers new possibilities and shows us what can be done. It wrestles with angels, looks impossibilities in the eye and winks. Hope springs eternal. Hope supersedes all good intentions.

Positive thinking can get you only so far. When that train of thought won't get you further, jump track and keep going by the power of God's grace. After all, you know Immanuel, God who is with us. Dare to believe that he has planned greater things right around the corner. Hold your loved ones before the throne and count on God's answer in their lives. Don't let your ability or inability to think your way around circumstances hold you back. Pray and rest. Then pray some more.

Barbara Johnson

We rejoice in the hope of the glory of God. Not only so, but we also rejoice in our sufferings, because we know that suffering produces perseverance; perseverance, character; and character, hope. And hope does not disappoint us, because God has poured out his love into our hearts by the Holy Spirit, whom he has given us.

ROMANS 5:2–5

MEDITATIONS ON FINDING HOPE

Because God wanted to make the unchanging nature of his purpose very clear to the heirs of what was promised, he confirmed it with an oath. God did this so that ... we who have fled to take hold of the hope offered to us may be greatly encouraged. We have this hope as an anchor for the soul, firm and secure.

HEBREWS 6:17–19

Why are you downcast, O my soul?
    Why so disturbed within me?
Put your hope in God,
    for I will yet praise him,
    my Savior and my God.

PSALM 42:5–6

Let us hold unswervingly to the hope we profess, for he who promised is faithful

HEBREWS 10:23

DON'T WORRY

*P*salm 139:16 says, "All the days ordained for me were written in your book before one of them came to be." I find that realization comforting. In fact, it could be a cheer-up thought. To recognize God's sovereign determining of the number of days each of us is to have on earth relieves me of nagging questions like, "If I had just done this, eaten that, not eaten that, stayed home, not stayed home … "

This is not some kind of Christian fatalism in which we assume it doesn't matter if we take health and safety precautions. On the contrary, Scripture says our bodies are the temples of the Holy Spirit, and we must respect them as well as do our part in preserving them. But tension is released in me as I remember that the number of my days is in his hands and not mine.

Marilyn Meberg

Commit your way to the LORD;
*   trust in him and he will do this:*
He will make your righteousness shine like the
dawn,
*   the justice of your cause like the noonday sun.*

PSALM 37:5–6

*I*n my opinion, there are no coincidences. When we make Jesus Christ the Lord of our lives, the Lord orders everything that happens to us. Psalm 37:23–24 says that when the Lord approves of a person's path, he makes that person's steps firm; even if the person stumbles, he won't fall because the Lord upholds him.

Thelma Wells

*D*avid prayed for "the wings of a dove" that he might fly far away from his problems and be at rest. I can get into that, can't you? At times I just want a fast, easy way out. I want to make my way to a hammock strung between two oaks at the water's edge where choirs of songbirds sing me to sleep.

Matthew tells us, "Look at the birds of the air; they do not sow or reap or store away in barns, and yet your heavenly Father feeds them. Are you not much more valuable than they?" What a lovely thought; he, too, is a bird-watcher. And to think his care and provision for us is even greater, for he is a people-watcher, too. How comforting.

Patsy Clairmont,

MEDITATIONS ON
NOT WORRYING

Are not five sparrows sold for two pennies? Yet not one of them is forgotten by God. Indeed, the very hairs of your head are all numbered. Don't be afraid; you are worth more than many sparrows.

LUKE 12:6–7

Do not worry, saying, "What shall we eat?" or "What shall we drink?" or "What shall we wear?" For the pagans run after all these things, and your heavenly Father knows that you need them. But seek first his kingdom and his righteousness, and all these things will be given to you as well.

MATTHEW 6:31–33

The Lord is near. Do not be anxious about anything.

PHILIPPIANS 4:5–6

Do not worry about tomorrow, for tomorrow will worry about itself. Each day has enough trouble of its own.

MATTHEW 6:34

HEALING POWER

*S*omeone said, "God will accept a broken heart, but he must have all the pieces." As he stitches those pieces back together, the moisture of tears softens and makes flexible his strong thread of healing in our lives. Big wet tears are part of the rich human experience. The people who weep unashamed are the same ones who live and love with their whole heart and soul. Those who mourn are those who have allowed themselves to feel real feelings because they care about other people.

Sometimes allowing yourself to cry is the scariest thing you'll ever do, and the bravest. It takes a lot of courage to face the facts, stare loss in the face, bare your heart, and let it bleed. But it is the only way to cleanse your wounds and prepare them for healing. God will take care of the rest.

God is offering himself to you daily, and the rate of exchange is fixed: your sins for his forgiveness, your hurt for his balm of healing, your sorrow for his joy. Give him your pain. Give him the guilt you feel, the heartaches that come to us all. They are part of living, but if you focus on Jesus Christ, he alone can ease your heartache. Then he uses us to dry the tears of others.

Barbara Johnson

*T*he story of the sick woman in Mark, chapter five, offers us encouragement. This woman was desperate, but she had heard about Jesus and her hope was renewed. She didn't want to call attention to herself—she had lived long with embarrassment—but she quietly worked her way through the crowd just to touch the hem of his cloak. I don't think Jesus had to turn around to know who had touched him. I think he did so to show her (and all those around him) how much he cared for her. I can picture him lifting her from her knees where she huddled in fear and, to her joy, calling her "Daughter." He looked her full in the eyes and ended her ordeal with his loving words. "Go in peace and be freed from your suffering."

Whatever problems we have, none are too personal to take to Jesus. He might offer us instant healing or inspiration to try a different approach or treatment to our health problems. We may indeed have to live with them for a long time. But in any case, we are his "daughters," and he offers hope of healing in every aspect of our lives.

Ruth DeJager

MEDITATIONS ON GOD'S HEALING POWER

The LORD said, "If you listen carefully to the voice of the LORD your God and do what is right in his eyes, if you pay attention to his commands and keep all his decrees, I will not bring on you any of the diseases ... for I am the LORD, who heals you."

EXODUS 15:26

Praise the LORD, O my soul;
    all my inmost being, praise his holy name.
Praise the LORD, O my soul,
    and forget not all his benefits—
who forgives all your sins
    and heals all your diseases,
who redeems your life from the pit
    and crowns you with love and compassion,
who satisfies your desires with good things
    so that your youth is renewed like the eagle's.

PSALM 103:1–5

TRUE PEACE OF MIND

*B*eing constantly courageous, at least in Christian terms, doesn't mean being tough. It means being tender toward God and his purposes. Great courage requires true surrender. God alone supplies the strength, the glory, the light by which the next step is revealed; he delivers peace and rest when the terrain appears unnavigable.

Debra Evans

*F*ollowing God presents many challenges. Admittedly, much in our lives is beyond our control. But isn't that where our greatest security lies? Relinquishing control to the God who is the master planner? Every morning we have a chance to choose again the path we will take that day. Choose God's path. Live the adventure only he can bring. Only then are we *absolutely* safe—forever.

*W*hen you're "walking in the dark," where do you look to discover which way to go? What do you trust? Whom do you trust? I turn first to some Scriptures I've learned, and I draw from my memory: "Trust in the LORD with all your heart and lean not on your own understanding" (Proverbs 3:5). I remember Jesus' words to his disciples: "Do not let your hearts be troubled. Trust in God; trust also in me" (John 14:1). And the apostle Paul's blessing to Rome's earliest Christians: "May the God of hope fill you with all joy and peace as you trust in him, so that you may overflow with hope by the power of the Holy Spirit" (Romans 15:13).

These memorable words help me get my bearings when I'm walking in the dark, when fear and doubt come creeping onto my path, into my heart. Thankfully, trust doesn't depend on our sensory perceptions for validation. Trust isn't about positive feelings—it's about childlike faith.

Debra Evans

*W*hen we reach the end of our strength, wisdom, and personal resources, we enter into the beginning of God's glorious provision. And that's a wondrous place to be.

Patsy Clairmont

MEDITATIONS ON HAVING TRUE PEACE OF MIND

Jesus said, "Everyone who hears these words of mine and puts them into practice is like a wise man who built his house on the rock. The rain came down, the streams rose, and the winds blew and beat against that house; yet it did not fall, because it had its foundation on the rock."

MATTHEW 7:24–25

The apostle Paul wrote, "Whatever is true, whatever is noble, whatever is right, whatever is pure, whatever is lovely, whatever is admirable—if anything is excellent or praiseworthy—think about such things. Whatever you have learned or received or heard from me, or seen in me—put it into practice. And the God of peace will be with you."

PHILIPPIANS 4:8–9

THE JOY OF THE LORD

*T*he wisdom and doctrine of Scripture teach that the experience of celebrating God is the core of worship. It is the quintessence of praise and thanksgiving—the most perfect manifestation of a heart that gratefully fellowships with the One who provides life and all the gifts of living. In fact, a grateful heart is not only the greatest virtue, it is the seed bed for all other virtues. When we are caught up into the celebration of God, there is neither room nor time for the invasion of negative living. As we rejoice before the Lord, as we serve him in the area of our calling, as we enter joyfully into our daily journey, as we give thanks to him for his kindness and faithfulness, we celebrate God.

Luci Swindoll

The LORD has done this,
  and it is marvelous in our eyes.
This is the day the LORD has made;
  let us rejoice and be glad in it.

PSALM 118:23–24

MEDITATIONS ON KNOWING THE JOY OF THE LORD

The apostle Paul wrote, "Rejoice in the Lord always. I will say it again: Rejoice!"

PHILIPPIANS 4:4

*"You will go out in joy
      and be led forth in peace;
the mountains and hills
      will burst into song before you,
and all the trees of the field
      will clap their hands,"
         declares the LORD.*

ISAIAH 55:12

Jesus said, "I have told you this so that my joy may be in you and that your joy may be complete."

JOHN 15:11

The joy of the LORD is your strength.

NEHEMIAH 8:10

PEACE TO THOSE
FAR AND NEAR

a group of us from Women of Faith went to West Africa. This was a very interesting and wonderful opportunity to take love, friendship, and peace to the other side of the globe, and to receive the same from the people who live there.

One morning as we were meeting for breakfast, Vikki Wells gave a short devotional from Acts 4:32: "All the believers were one in heart and mind. No one claimed that any of his possessions was his own, but they shared everything they had."

Everybody standing in that circle, she said, was just the same in Christ. There were no differences or barriers. There were no degrees of separation because of race, color, status, background, possessions. *I love that.* We were indeed one great fellowship.

I remember thinking at that moment, *I'm over here on the other side of the globe, yet I feel so at home. At peace. Why do I feel this way? What is it?* It didn't take long to realize that "it" was spiritual companionship and shared passion for the same Savior.

THE GOSPEL OF *Peace*

*T*he sweetest part of the relationship we have with the Almighty is telling others about what we've learned and that they, too, can enjoy oneness with God. They can know his love by becoming intimately acquainted with his Son, Jesus. Witnessing is not some hocus-pocus thing. It's simply showing up in life every day, expressing what God has done for us, how he's met us along the way, and how he can do the same for the person with whom we're sharing.

I realize it's not possible for everybody to travel to a foreign country to share the gospel. That's not the point of Jesus' "great commission." The point is to simply go. Anywhere. Talk to anybody about the friendship God offers through the redemptive work of his Son on the cross. We don't need money or a passport, a vaccination or a plane ticket to fulfill the commission Jesus gave us. What we need is a heart of love, which causes us to reach out in the first place.

We are commanded to introduce people to Christ, train them in the way they should live under his love and protection, instruct them in his teachings. When we do this, he has promised us his constant presence. What could be more loving and fulfilling than such a powerful assignment and such a personal promise?

Luci Swindoll

MEDITATIONS ON BRINGING PEACE TO THOSE FAR AND NEAR

How beautiful on the mountains
*   are the feet of those who bring good news,*
who proclaim peace,
*   who bring good tidings,*
*   who proclaim salvation,*
who say to Zion,
*   "Your God reigns!"*

ISAIAH 52:7

"Peace, peace, to those far and near,"
*   says the LORD.*

ISAIAH 57:19

Stand firm then, with the belt of truth buck-
led around your waist, with the breastplate of
righteousness in place, and with your feet fit-
ted with the readiness that comes from the
gospel of peace.

EPHESIANS 6:14–15

Bell, Valerie. *A Well-Tended Soul*. Grand Rapids: Zondervan, 1996.

Buchanan, Sue. *I'm Alive and the Doctor's Dead*. Grand Rapids: Zondervan, 1994.

Clairmont, Patsy, Barbara Johnson, Marilyn Meberg, Luci Swindoll, Sheila Walsh, Thelma Wells. *Boundless Love*. Grand Rapids: Zondervan, 2001.

Clairmont, Patsy, Barbara Johnson, Marilyn Meberg, Luci Swindoll, Sheila Walsh, Thelma Wells. *Extravagant Grace*. Grand Rapids: Zondervan, 2000.

Clairmont, Patsy, Barbara Johnson, Marilyn Meberg, Luci Swindoll, Sheila Walsh, Thelma Wells. *Outrageous Joy*. Grand Rapids: Zondervan, 1999.

Clairmont, Patsy, Barbara Johnson, Marilyn Meberg, Luci Swindoll, Sheila Walsh, Thelma Wells. *OverJoyed*. Grand Rapids: Zondervan, 1999.

Evans, Debra. *Women of Character*. Grand Rapids: Zondervan, 1996.

———— *Women of Courage*. Grand Rapids: Zondervan, 1999.

Experiencing God's Presence. Grand Rapids: Zondervan, 1998.

Walsh, Sheila. *Living Fearlessly*. Grand Rapids: Zondervan, 2001.

The Women of Faith Study Bible. Grand Rapids: Zondervan, 2001.

The Women's Devotional Bible. Grand Rapids: Zondervan, 1990.

The Women's Devotional Bible 2. Grand Rapids: Zondervan, 1995